I0620625

There Is No Place Like Dome

All attempts have been made to preserve the stories of the events, locales and conversations contained in this collection as the author remembers them. The author reserves the right to have changed the names of individuals and places if necessary and may have changed some identifying characteristics and details such as physical properties, occupations and places of residence in order to maintain their anonymity.

Published by St. Petersburg Press
St. Petersburg, FL
www.stpetersburgpress.com

Copyright ©2025

All rights reserved. No part of this publication may be reproduced, distributed, or transmitted in any form or by any means, including photocopying, recording or other electronic or mechanical methods, without the prior written permission of the publisher, except in the case of brief quotations embodied in critical reviews and certain other noncommercial uses permitted by copyright law. For permission requests contact St. Petersburg Press at www.stpetersburgpress.com.

Design and composition by St. Petersburg Press and Isa Crosta

Cover design by Kelly Reynolds

Print ISBN: 978-1-964239-17-0
eBook ISBN: 978-1-964239-18-7

First Edition

There Is No Place Like Dome

*A Fan Host's Unofficial View from
the Top of the Trop
To the Stands with the Fans*

by
Bruce Reynolds

A unique perspective inside one of baseball's most unique ball-parks. A book full of stories to enjoy long after the Trop becomes a cherished memory.

Nate Kurant, in-game host Tropicana Field

Contents

Throwing Out
The First Pitch:

To all Fan Hosts (past and present) who have given fans an All-Star experience while they came to The Trop to watch Rays baseball.

Rays Up!

The views, thoughts and opinions expressed in this book are mine, the author. They do not necessarily reflect those of The Tampa Bay Rays Organization.

1

Opener

October 19, 2008—The Tampa Bay Rays were one out from going to the World Series! The Devil Rays, which dropped the "Devil" at the beginning of the season, were ready to accomplish the unimaginable. A franchise that had never finished at .500 in their existence, much less made the playoffs, was on the verge of history. David Price delivered the pitch and Jed Lowrie of the Red Sox hit a ground ball to second baseman Aki Iwamura, who cleanly fielded the ball and stepped on second base. The impossible just became possible. THE RAYS WERE GOING TO THE WORLD SERIES! 40,473 fans erupted in euphoria. Everyone in Tampa Bay, whether they attended the game or watched it on TV, remembered where they were when that final out was made!

This was my very first season as a Fan Host (usher) working at Tropicana Field. No question, I remember where I was … on a cruise ship in the Pacific Ocean off the coast of San Francisco (*more on that later*).

Fan Fest of 2008 brought my wife, Jeanette, and I wandering through Tropicana Field, just taking in the sights of the day. I had been a baseball fan since "having a catch with my dad" (*Field of Dreams*) when I was a little boy growing up in Baltimore. I have great memories of watching Brooks Robinson, Frank Robinson, Jim Palmer, Eddie Murray, and Cal Ripken Jr. at both Memorial

Stadium and Oriole Park at Camden Yards. (Truth be told, for many years, I had a massive Oriole memorabilia collection, which included autographed bats, jerseys, and a locker! Oh yeah, I even owned an usher's hat— *how ironic*). Back in '08, Ripken had retired, and my allegiance to the Orioles had begun to fade. The Rays were now becoming my hometown team. I had season tickets during their first year in 1998. Little did I know that, less than ten years later, I would become a Fan Host just a few sections away from where those seats were located.

Early on, mixing baseball with fun (back left).

Walking around during Fan Fest 2008, my wife and I noticed a sign-up for people who were interested in being ushers (we did not know the term *Fan Host* yet). Thinking it might be a fun way to be ambassadors for our community through baseball, we signed up, believing we would be volunteers. Later, finding out we would get paid was a pleasant shock.

These past 16 years have only increased my love of "America's

Past Time" while also becoming emotionally involved in the lives of fans and fellow Fan Hosts who have become my baseball "family."

My pulse raced as I watched game 162 unfold, only to have my heart broken seeing Drew Rasmussen's perfect game lost in the 9th inning. The euphoria I experience with fans after an amazing walk-off win counters the heartache over hearing some of their heartbreak from their personal lives. Through the years I have attended weddings, as well as funerals, with these "family members."

I got chills watching (even though I knew ahead of time) an unsuspecting teenage girl throw out the first pitch to an unknown player in catcher's gear, only to discover his identity to be her dad, who had come home early from the military to surprise her and her family. Also, there was the night that a drunken fan thought it would be a good idea to sucker punch Raymond, the team mascot, and knock him to the ground.

Within these pages, walk with me through the *vomitory*—yep, that's what the passageway that allows people to enter or leave the field view of Tropicana Field is called. (For those of us who work there, we refer to this as coming through the *vom* to the bowl.) *See, this book is educational!*

In reading this book, you will visualize the game of baseball through the eyes of somebody who thinks he has seen it all, until something either on or off the field surprises me again. Truly, *There Is No Place Like Dome.*

Between Innings

A break in the action

Baseball is unique in that there are built in breaks throughout the game. Other than a team calling time out, most other sports pause when it is a commercial break.

For years, the NFL employed a representative to step onto the field to let the officials know it was time to break for a commercial or to play on after the change of possession. He would take a step or two out onto the field, wearing a large oversized "oven mitt," usually bright orange or red, that was placed across his chest to the opposite shoulder so that he could be spotted quickly. In more recent years, that has been replaced with the network television coordinator wearing orange sleeves, raising his arm to indicate the game to be halted. The NFL requires sixteen commercial breaks per game, eight each half.

But in baseball, there are breaks at the middle and the end of each inning as players either take the field or come to bat.

Did you know that up until the mid-1950s, players left their gloves in the field near their position to pick them up when they returned the next inning? *(This was told to me by Bobby Richardson, New York Yankee second baseman who played back then.)*

One of the things I find most fascinating as a Fan Host is to watch the unique tendencies that fans have when coming to a game. Often, whether a person comes alone, with someone else, or even as part of a larger group, they all want to do the same thing at the same time. They want their picture taken, which is certainly understandable. However, a lot of fans wait until after the half-inning, when the game has started again, to stand up either in the aisle or go down to the dugout to pose! We have at least 16 half-innings when the game has stopped to take that shot. But somehow, fans think once the game has started again, with the action behind them, is then a good time for that picture, meanwhile blocking other people's view of the game! (I find myself partially smiling while shaking my head, as this scenario is repeated numerous times throughout a game.)

In this book I want to provide you with some *Inning Breaks* between each chapter that have provided me a lot of fun through the years. Starting after the 2012 season, for the benefit of my fellow Fan Hosts, if not at least for my entertainment, I have written a poem summarizing the previous Rays baseball season. Most years I have read the annual "masterpiece" during our season-ending holiday party, or to start the new season at our pre-season training (Rays University.) What follows the chapters are some excerpts from these poems. If you are a Rays fan, some of the lines might prod your memory of those past seasons. These *odes* are certainly not any piece of great poetry. Probably my former English teachers and professors would cringe knowing I was once their student. Hopefully these poem excerpts will trigger a flashback, or at least a smile, now and then. I like to call each poem a *Reynolds Rap*. (Author's note: there is a lot of this type of *humor* ahead. You have been warned!)

Stepping Out Of The Box

For those of you old enough to remember, there was a player named Mike Hargrove (1974-1985) who seemed to always step out of the batter's box after each pitch. He had a routine of adjusting his jersey, helmet, batting gloves, cleats etc. that was infuriating to the opposing pitcher. He had the nickname of "The Human Rain Delay" in light of his routine at the plate.

Throughout the book you will see random postings of *Stepping Out of the Box* at the end of chapters. These brief statements (I have to watch out for the new time clock) are *some* of the passing thoughts I have had through the years while working at The Trop. *Don't deliberate too long or the umpire might call a strike on you.*

Stepping out of the Box: *What would happen if a player threw his drinking cup on the floor at home and left it there as he does in the dugout?*

2012 Season Poem (excerpt)
90-72 (3rd in AL East)

Opening Day is always for the fan
Carlos drove them crazy with a 1st inning slam.

Early on the talk was about the new stadium in Miami
Then we all groaned when Longo injured his hammy.

Constantly playing the AL East was quite a task
The Rays countered early on with a Gladiator mask.

For a time, we had Allen, Matsui, and then "Tatman"
But don't forget Rhymes, who claimed he was Batman.

During "Dog Days" there was a concern about their dung
But hey it was Astro's master that won the Cy Young!

Having Luke Scott around was no bother
Except when the Star Wars fans cheered "Luke I am your father!"

We were used to hearing Dave/Andy say "Shields winds and "fires"
But now we find ourselves cheering for Wil Myers.

Spring Training

Entering my "rookie" year as a Fan Host in 2008, I knew a lot about baseball but little about what it took to be an "usher." (After all, weren't ushers the "killjoys" that would not let you sneak down into better seats either before or once the game started?) I am sure they did not notice me ... well maybe ... while I was still an Orioles fan, I also wanted to stay true to the hometown team. I would wear an Orioles hat along with a Devil Rays shirt! (Hmmm ... come to think of it, I still see fans today doing the same thing when their two teams are playing at The Trop.)

Before the season begins, Fan Hosts attend Rays University (*Rays U*). This focused time on being prepared to enhance a fan's experience lasts anywhere from 1-3 evenings, depending on the year. What can seem like a mindless job, in that all you do is check tickets and then watch baseball, is far from reality. On any given game there are close to 150-200 Fan Hosts fulfilling a variety of responsibilities—from scanning tickets (on the phone these days ... paper tickets are rarely seen anymore) to operating an elevator or escalator to supervising the crowds visiting the Rays tank (yep real Rays that swim in water) to answering an assortment of questions at Guest Services to providing assistance to our wheelchair folks (Rolling Rays) to hosting fans in a variety of clubs throughout the stadium, and much more.

During my first Rays U, one of the biggest lessons, one which I am still learning, was to familiarize ourselves with the building itself. The Trop's structure and angle creates an assortment of challenges to find your way around. I had to learn to be able to succinctly and correctly answer a fan's question regarding the closest restroom, elevator, or ATM. We don't have as much of a need for ATMs since every transaction is done by card or your phone; therefore, the only Cash that is recognized at The Trop is in The Rays dugout, and he manages the team! (*Remember, I warned you!*)

As I look back over my 16 years as a Fan Host, the main principle I first learned at Rays U has stayed with me today. As a Fan Host, I really have no impact on what takes place on the field, but I have a lot to do with a fan's experience during the game. Regardless of the final score, I want to do all that I can for the fan to have a memorable time. Hopefully they will have enjoyed themselves, so much so that they want to return for another game. To that end, the Rays management has been very tolerant in allowing me to be myself when having fun with the fans, which has included a variety of costumes and gimmicks. (*See chapter 10 "Getting My Head In The Game" and chapter 12 "Alternate Unis."*)

I officially graduated from Rays U on April 3, 2008, with a diploma which still hangs on my wall at home. Each year I return to be reminded of my focus and purpose, as well as to glean something new that will make me a better Fan Host.

Since I have been around so long, often I am asked back to come to speak to the new Fan Hosts about what to possibly expect once the season starts. I try to be honest about my experiences and share my "hits, runs and errors." You will read about many of these in the coming chapters. Truly as Fan Hosts, we are the *Face of the Franchise*. Obviously, the fans come to see the players, but Fan Hosts are the first people they are greeted by as they arrive and the last ones as they leave.

As Fan Hosts, we learn to take responsibility.

When speaking at Rays U with first year Fan Hosts, I often come with a variety of hats to help describe our role. There is a *Fireman's hat,* where we put out "fires" that range from a disagreement among fans to someone who hurt their hand trying to catch a foul ball to a fan who inadvertently dropped their food, and so much more.

Once one of those "fires" came from a frantic woman who approached me before a game. She was not sitting in my section but still came over to me and somehow knew my name. She desperately needed my help as there was a "wild beast" underneath her seat. I asked her to repeat the phrase and she said exactly the same thing. Naturally, I went with her to see what I could do to potentially tame this "wild beast." As we approached her seat cautiously, she pointed underneath it where there was a crumbled-up sweatshirt. I then asked if the "wild beast" was under the sweatshirt, to which she shook her head, yes. When I questioned what was under her sweatshirt, she told me it was a bat. (At that time The Trop had recently undergone some construction which had disturbed a number of bats that we often saw outside as were leaving at the end of the game, but few had been spotted inside.) After discovering the identity of the "wild beast," and to lighten the moment, my sense of humor was ready to kick in. I was so close to telling this distraught woman that the Rays use bats every game when they hit. Something told me that she would not appreciate my humor (*I seem to get that often*) at this time and it would be a waste of good material to share it with her. Yes, the bat was removed by stadium personnel.

These "fires" can become much more intense than overcoming "*wild beasts*." We have assisted children who have been lost from their parents. This is a stressful situation for both until they are reunited. More recently we have had some of our senior fans "lose their way" and struggle to find their family or group and the location of their seat. (TIP: since tickets are now electronic, ask the holder of all the tickets to take a screenshot once everyone has entered The Trop and then text it to each member of the group. This way the entire group now has a copy of their own ticket.)

Fan Hosts also wear any number of other hats during a game, to further enhance the Fan Experience. At Rays U, I put on a *Train Conductor's* hat to explain that we are often giving directions as well as checking tickets. *(On August 14, 2010, I wore my Conductors hat the night we had a post-game concert with the group*

Train. Remember "Hey Soul Sister?") Yes, we do check tickets, which is not only a part of our job, but also out of respect to other fans who sit in the same area. People often think if the seat is empty during the game, it is no big deal to sit there—it doesn't hurt anybody. Well, it does "hurt" the fan who paid the full price for that ticket. Usually, the people who are trying to sneak in have not paid nearly as much. Just about any other ticketed performance does not let you sit anywhere you please. You are to sit in the seat that is printed on your ticket.

I have had numerous fans come thank me for asking people who do not have that particular ticket to move. Those who belong often feel "cheated" or disrespected by those who try to sneak in. There are also season ticket holders who are quite "protective" of their seat(s) if they are not there. For instance, perhaps they have gone up to The Draft Room which is exclusively for season ticket holders for a couple of innings, with the intent of returning to their seat. Others have not attended a game but watch it on TV and become disturbed if someone else is seated in their seat. Often season ticket holders have given their seat(s) away that night and they will tell me ahead of time of the switch. Regardless of the ticket plan, if a person has paid for a seat for a designated number of games, when possible, it becomes my responsibility to be sure that seat is only occupied by the authorized "owner."

You might find this hard to believe, but sometimes fans will lie to me about the seat they are sitting in. When I ask them to show me their ticket, it often has become "lost." Think about it, that is hard to do these days since your ticket is on your phone. (An amazing number of phone batteries die in The Trop once fans enter the stadium!) Then when the ticket is shown to me, they say "I must have misread it." It's hard for me to *understand* how you can get section 217 row E, seat 8, confused with section 118 row BB and seat 2!

We also wear *Hard Hats. (Yep, I have one of those, too with a Rays decal on the front. I will often wear it during the playoffs, telling people who ask that The Rays still have work to do. There have been Labor Day games when I have worn it as well.)* Please understand when I say, I love being a Fan Host and it is a lot of fun. Along with that, however comes the understanding that it is a job. Regardless of where a Fan Host is positioned during the game, they are working. Each area of the stadium has its own unique responsibilities that must be addressed in a professional manner.

As a Fan Host, we are scheduled to arrive at The Trop a half-hour before the gates open, which varies depending on the day of the week. We receive a 20- minute break, during which we head to our break area, hopefully sit down, eat, and possibly go to the restroom during that time. That is not a lot of time when you consider that baseball (even with the new pitch clock) is the only major sport other than golf that does not have a clock. Therefore, a game can last, say a little over two hours. Even some 9 inning games go over 3 hours along with the possibility of extra innings. Afterwards, depending on the area you are stationed, you are still working 20-45 minutes once the game ends. Then there are special games like Sundays when kids get to run the bases, or a concert night and your shift is extended approximately another hour-and-a-half to two hours.

I write this not for sympathy, but for people to understand that being a Fan Host is a job. Through the years our pay has increased, which of course is a … *Raise Up!* (Yep)

Often a Fan Host wears a *Top Hat* (I do own one of these, too but use it only for when speaking to the "rookies"). Regardless if the Top Hat can be seen or not, we at times do perform "magic" for the fans. For each game, as we enter our locker room, there is a sign that hangs over the entrance:

Sometimes the "work" consists of celebrating a Rays victory with the fans!

"Energizing our fans through the magic of baseball."

I have witnessed numerous magical moments of Rays baseball: Arozarena stealing home in the playoffs, the incredible relay from Kiermaier to Adames to d'Arnaud getting the Astros' Jose Altuve out at the plate in the 2019 post season come immediately to mind.

But we also have a *few tricks up our sleeves* that at times we are able to perform and significantly impact a fan's experience. Some years ago, a young woman who faithfully attended many games, often engaged me in conversation. We conversed on numerous occasions on anything from, obviously, baseball to life in general. One night she informed me that I would not be seeing her around The Trop for a while.

As I asked her why and she told me she was going to have hip surgery, and that it was rare enough it could not be performed in the States. She was headed overseas for the surgery and she was leaving the next day or two. As we talked, I could tell she was concerned about her surgery along with sadness for not being able to attend Rays games for some time. A few innings later I went to her seat, hoping to cheer her up. I told her we at the Rays would be thinking of her while she was gone and hoping she, too would be thinking of us as well. At that I placed in her hand a ball I was able to secure. As she looked up, I told her to know of our love, as well as to look at the ball to be a reminder of our support.

A few months later I saw her again from a distance, walking toward me without a hint of a limp and the brightest smile. I welcomed her back to The Trop. She then opened her purse to pull out the ball I had given her. She began to tell me how well the surgery went. Her story continued to unfold as she relayed that she had taken the ball with her overseas. Once she got to her hospital room she placed the ball on the night stand beside her bed. Each time she looked at the ball it reminded her of The Rays organization and our support. After surgery, she also took it with her as she went to physical therapy. Obviously, she was thrilled with the way everything went, as well as now being able to again enjoy her Rays.

Yes, we at times do wear invisible top hats that enable us to do some magic. Those special moments in the stands with fans are just as memorable and emotional as those unforgettable plays on the field. It is those *magical* times that when they come to mind, make me realize how fortunate I am to be a Fan Host. I find it rewarding to be able to help energize our fans through the magic of Rays baseball.

Once *Rays U* (our spring training) is complete, we know Opening Day is not too far away. Opening Day in baseball is unlike the beginning of any other sports season. Of course, there is the hope of every team and their fans that this is "our year." Regardless of how last season ended, 29 out of the 30 teams were disappointed because they did not win the World Series. For years now there has been a movement started that Opening Day should be a holiday (similar to the perspective that the day after the Super Bowl, people should not have to go to school or work). With baseball that gets to be a bit trickier in that not every team starts their season on the same day. Also, what if you start the season on the road, it could be up to a week or so before you have your home opener.

Speaking of openers, yeah I know it is not the same (but hey it's my book lol), one of the great giveaways the Rays offered occurred on April 20, 2019.

The Rays were the first team to be innovative in having a relief pitcher start the game as the team's *opener*. Back in 2018 they were highly criticized by the media as well as some of the players around the league. You don't hear too much of that talk anymore, do you? I digress but on that Saturday night in 2019 against the Red Sox, all fans, while supplies lasted, were given a Ryne Stanek (who was often our opener) bottle opener! That was classic!

Back to Opening Day … once the gates open the excitement begins. The best description I can give is that it is like going back to school after summer vacation. You see fans that you have not seen since last season. There are plenty of hugs and smiles as we interact with "our baseball family" after a sustained absence. There is a lot of catching up going on as well as anticipation of a new season. Plenty of fans have gone through months of "baseball withdrawal." The MLB Network (as good as it is), or replays of memorable games from last season, just don't seem to be enough any longer once the end of March arrives.

For me, one of the most impressive aspects of Opening Day happens long before the gates are opened. We, as Fan Hosts, all gather in one large briefing (200+) to unite our efforts as well as to "Rays Up,"to begin another baseball season. During that briefing just about every year we have the same speaker come to thank us for what we do for the organization. Stu Sternberg, the majority owner of The Rays comes to speak to us often with Presidents Matt Silverman and Brian Auld.

With all the demands on the time of these gentlemen, they make time for us, Fan Hosts. Obviously, I do not know this for sure, but of the other 29 owners, I wonder how many of them on their home opener are doing the same thing? Their presence and words are not necessary or expected, but still they come, and that speaks volumes year after year.

Stepping out of the box: *Why if a run scores due to a pitcher's error? Is the run unearned?*

2013 Season Poem (excerpt)
92-71 (2nd in AL East)
ALDS lost 3-1

At times Rodney was Fernan-NO...something was wrong
Me? I thought he was allergic to the gong!

Myer's first at bat at The Trop was a mammoth jack
The middle homer of a back-to-back to back

It was great to see Price come off the DL throwing zeroes
But dog-gone it, wasn't it funny that his first game was against
the Astros!

Twice in three days a Lobaton walk-off was part of Maddon's
scheme.
His reward besides two victories was lots of ice cream.

Chris Archer is well-read and thoughtful with each retort
While some of us Fan Hosts wore striped socks when he pitched
for *Arch-support.*

DeJesus came at the end of the trade deadline in our push for
1st place
Did you know his wife Kim, like Longo's Jaime, competed on The
Amazing Race?

Pre-Game

Fan Hosts arrive long before the gates open. We have our own parking lot and gate where we enter The Trop. In the bowels of the stadium, we head to our sanctuary which we call "Wardrobe."

Wardrobe is our locker room, along with a break area for those who choose to use it. It is where we get our jerseys and scan our credentials to check in and out for work. There have been times that the scanner has not worked as well as other times. One day I was attempting to scan in and was getting quite frustrated that my ID badge card was not being read. After a few unsuccessful attempts, I realized that I was placing my badge under the hand soap dispenser right next to the scanner. Luckily no one was around to see my "error," but I felt I needed to "come clean" in telling you. (Don't say I didn't warn you.)

Though The Trop might be "empty," there is still much taking place both on and off the field before the gates are opened. Depending on where you are positioned, there are responsibilities to be carried out so that the fans will have a memorable experience at the game. We meet in various parts of The Trop with those we work with to go over our responsibilities for the upcoming game. These briefings are facilitated by our "Leads"- fellow Fan Hosts who take on many more responsibilities in the area of The Trop they oversee. They should permanently wear one of those "Fireman's Hats.". Throughout the game, they are constantly addressing issues and crises, in essence *putting out fires*. For all my years working on 1st base, I have been fortunate to serve under some great "Leads." They have been supportive and encouraging, as well as knowledgeable. Yet they have not micromanaged us as Fan Hosts. They have allowed us to do our jobs, as well as to be ourselves, which as you will discover, that is saying a lot when it comes to me. They have my gratitude and appreciation, along with being so glad I am not doing their jobs.

During our pre-game briefing times, we are informed on any number of issues, from estimated attendance to unique things happening for that particular game. This could be a special presentation, like who might be throwing out the first pitch, to a promotional give away that we should be aware and informed about.

As our briefing on 1st base concludes each game, we are dismissed with the same send off. It began with our Lead, Ken Jones, reciting it. We have now done this for years before departing to our assigned areas. One of us is asked to give this "benediction." The farewell is a line from the 1974 movie "Blazing Saddles" (yea some of us are that old) delivered by Harvey Korman. *"Now go do that voodoo, that you do, so well."* It has been delivered with a variety of accents and emphasis, but it is a fun way for all of us to be prepared for the upcoming game.

First base "voo-doers."

Besides employees, one of the few people allowed in the stands before the gates open are scouts from other teams. They sit and watch as batting practice (BP) takes place, often alone, but at times a group of them will sit together. At the latest, once BP ends, they leave their seats and their pre-game responsibilities are finished. Year after year as I watched these men do their jobs, I wondered what in the world could they possibly be studying? Finally, I went up to one of them and asked, "What are you looking for in watching BP?" The scout told me two very interesting things. First, he said he watched to see if players were really hurt and if so, how badly. Secondly, and this one really got my attention, the scout was watching to see what kind of teammate a player was with the other players. Did he hang around the batting cage to joke and talk with the other guys, or was he often by himself? Did it seem that the rest of the team had little to do with him? I am not sure I would have gotten either of those responses correct even on multiple choice, but once hearing them they both made a lot of sense.

Once the gates open, many fans like to arrive early for the game for a variety of reasons. Some just like to avoid the rush, so they enjoy roaming around long before they head to their seats. Others come to see BP, which at times can be disappointing. At The

Trop, just like the rest of MLB, the home team always takes batting practice first. Usually by the time the gates open, The Rays are done and have already exited the field. Many fans are immediately saddened once they find out that the players they came to see have already finished with their pre-game routines.

Also, there is the disappointment of arriving early to see neither of the teams take BP. Usually that is on a "get-away day," meaning when at the conclusion of the game, teams are leaving to go out of town. They possibly travel back home (visiting team) or head to their next city for a game the following day.

Keep in mind if you are coming to a Sunday game (which is one of my favorite days to work but more on that later), almost always there is no BP. Maybe some infield work gets done in a shorter time schedule but normally the field is not being used until game time.

During the 2013 season, The Rays introduced a unique way to announce the starting of the game. To go along with their theme song of *Bang a Gong* (Get It On), there was literally an actual gong installed on the concourse in right field. There was a designated "ringer" who would strike the gong with a mallet to let everyone know it was game time. (I guess that was the first *strike* of the game.)

At the conclusion of the Rays BP, before the fans entered, some of the pitchers would have a contest as they walked off the field. From around the bullpen area, they would try to "bang a gong" with a baseball, with varying degrees of success. Think about it … that is a pretty good distance to throw, much less to be accurate in hitting the gong. If those guys who were professionals in throwing and accuracy couldn't do it consistently, imagine any of us attempting it.

(I think it would have been fun trying.) It was an entertaining conclusion to batting practice.

There can be some satisfaction by arriving early, even if The Rays have finished taking BP (beyond getting that first hot dog and or beverage). Upon entering the bowl of The Trop, you can still hear the unmistakable sound of the crack of the bat. This, of course, means the visiting team is hitting and balls are soaring all over the field. Many fans arrive early to hopefully catch a batting practice ball hit into the outfield seats. The competition can be quite fierce among fans trying to snag one of those cherished dingers.

A few times I have been assigned to work the game in the outfield. Besides the view, it is a whole different ball game (pun intended) out there. The aspect I did not like the most was batting practice. Those "homers" are flying out there often in rapid succession, unlike a game when a ball arrives once in a while. As a Fan Host I found that during BP I had to have my head on a swivel for my safety as well as for the fans. For a season or two, Fan Hosts who worked out there had whistles which they blew when a ball was headed in that direction.

Speaking of batting practice home runs, you need to check out *Zack Hample* (zackhample.com). Zack travels the world to ballparks throughout the baseball season. He has the art of catching BP homers, and other baseballs down to a science. Through his "career," Zack has been in over 63 MLB stadiums and has caught over 12,000 baseballs! (Notably he caught Mike Trout's 1st career homer, as well as A-Rod's 3,000th hit.) Zack is known around the country by fans, and even certain players and coaches, on his quest for baseballs. He knows over 30 languages in how to ask a player for a ball! Zack also seeks out unique baseballs that have special logos on them to add to his collection. One of the things I respect about him is that he often gives the baseballs he has caught away to other fans, just about exclusively to children. He has made over 20 videos on his trips to The Trop throughout the years. In 2018, Zack appeared on the pregame show with Rich Hollenberg and Orestes Destrade. Look for him if you are in the outfield during BP. You never know when he will show up. He is quite approachable while taking time for a picture and or an autograph.

Scan QR Code with your phone to watch Zach's interaction with The Rays media

Once fans begin to enter The Trop, regardless where we are working, our Fan Host antennas go up. We are attempting to be in tune with fans to assist and/or anticipate their requests or needs. There are tickets to be scanned as people arrive through the gates. This can be an even greater challenge depending on the gate, the expected attendance as well as the weather.

As I mentioned there are a select group of fans that love to arrive as early as possible, yet there are others who, for any number of reasons, show up almost just before the first pitch. That increases the pressure on those scanning the tickets as well as those like myself who are assisting fans to find their seats. Before each game there are fans who are not that familiar with The Trop, so finding their seat can be a challenge. Often people will ask me if I can help them, or I will walk up to them when they seem to be a little *lost*, offering my assistance.

My go-to response almost all the time is to first tell the fan that they are close. As they often give me that puzzled look, *I tell them you are close … you are in the ballpark!* The responses (or lack of) can vary greatly. Some laugh out loud and ask me how many times have I used that line? Others give me what I call "the courtesy laugh." Believe me when I say I have lost count on how many of those I have received times in my life, an occupational hazard. Then there are others who give me a blank look and have no response at all; the line went completely over their head. (To myself I think, I just wasted good material.) Before you "judge" me, you should know that I have heard other employees, as well as security personnel, use "my line". My wife used to ask me if I really am still saying that. I reply as often as I can. She has stopped asking.

During pre-game, a significant amount of time, especially as we get close to first pitch, is spent assisting fans to find their seats. When a couple comes to me and shows me their tickets, I tell them how many rows down and then whether to turn to the right or the left, depending on their section. As they begin to proceed down the steps, I say to the person following the "leader," to follow them and if you get lost, blame them. Many of those followers (usually spouses) smile and say in some form or another, I already have done that numerous times before.

Now if a larger group (four or more) arrives, I tell the second person the same joke, but then tell the last person in line that in these sections, the first one down buys!

Also, if you are coming with a group and you are all sitting together, keep this in mind. You do NOT have to sit in your exact numbered seat. So many times, I see a group get down to their row and then it becomes bedlam because somebody is ready to sit in seat #4 but their ticket says #7.

As fans walk by, regardless of the team they are rooting for, I have found myself saying to them, "Enjoy the game, and if you can't enjoy the game, enjoy the air conditioning." That usually provokes a response of a smile or a chuckle, while others get "spiritual" and say AMEN!

During the time before the game starts, I have found it to be a great opportunity to converse with fans about any number of topics, from baseball to much more significant life issues. One game I noticed a woman sitting by herself on the end of the row anxiously looking down toward the dugout. As I approached her to ask if there was anything I could do, she smiled and said she was watching her son down near the field trying to get an autograph. While beginning to joke with her regarding kids pursuing autographs along with the responsibility of being a mom in watching her son, she got much more somber. She began to tear up a bit as she started to tell me about her son. He was 12 at the time and was suffering from a degenerating eye disease that would eventually end in him losing his sight all together.

I listened intently as she told me of her son's love of The Rays and how he enjoyed coming to the game. She went on to say she knew they would not be able to attend many more games due to his condition, so she wanted to bring him to as many games as she could now. Their seats were about halfway up the section behind the Rays dugout, which was all that she could afford. Even though they were good seats, this mom realized her son would still struggle to see the game. Needless to say, I was touched and stunned as this mom opened up her heart to share her story. I told her I was sorry for her and her son and then excused myself.

Through a series of events that we as Fan Hosts can sometimes do, we were able to again perform some of our "magic." We had the opportunity to move this mom and her son down next to the dugout, obviously much closer to the field, to some unused seats for that game. (We at times know of season ticket holders who tell us of games they will not be attending and for us to feel free to seat other people in their seats.) I later found out he was given a player's batting gloves to cap off his night. That young boy saw a baseball game as he had probably never seen one before, and most likely ever would see one again.

Obviously, this type of situation cannot often be duplicated. But for that one evening, a pre-game discussion led to a memorable encounter for not only that mother and son, but for me as well. It was another reminder of what a great opportunity I have in my job to help create an unforgettable fan experience.

Before the game starts, there is the pre-game tradition of throwing out the 1st pitch, of which I have seen quite a few (including the military dad catching for his daughter mentioned earlier). There have been celebrities, athletes, as well as special guests that have received the honor. Some of those pitches have been grooved from 60' 6" while others have dribbled in from far shorter distances.

Then there was a game in 2012, when Guy Boucher, the Lightning coach at the time, used a hockey stick for a slap shot first pitch that catcher Stephen Vogt (new manager of the Guardians) caught while in a goalies stance, complete with stick and mask (catcher's).

IF you ever get the opportunity to throw out the first pitch, may I offer you a few suggestions from one who has probably seen about 1000 of them. YIKES, have I been there that long!

1. *Don't go to the mound if you know you can't throw it that far. Standing in front of the mound is far less embarrassing than throwing a ball that dribbles to the plate.*

2. *Have your phone with you. Be prepared to take a quick selfie before throwing. When are you going to get another opportunity like this ever again?*

3. *Bring along a pen. Have whoever catches your pitch to sign the ball once it is returned to you. Regardless if it is a player or a mascot, still a cool keepsake.*

In addition to the first pitch, there are also a couple of other matters that take place before the game begins. The Rays are very sensitive about their young fans being "involved" in the game. (More on kids running the bases later.) Before each game, a child is selected to take the game ball and the resin bag out to the mound. (Honorary Bat Kid). Then another child gets to shout in the microphone after the players are on the field, "PLAY BALL!" (Play Ball Kid.) This obviously is a big deal for the child as well as their family members who are watching.

My youngest two grandsons (Shiloh and Gideon) were asked during the 2023 season to perform these tasks. After 16 years, having "one of my own" was very exciting. They both were pumped to go onto the field with my wife. Well until reality hit my youngest, Shiloh, of where he was, and he immediately became shy. Gideon looked confident as he ran on the field, jumping over the baseline as instructed to deliver the ball and resin bag. As he left the mound and raced off, he turned and waved to the crowd! I laughed out loud as I was recording all of this on my phone from the Jumbotron. Then came Shiloh's turn to shout those immortal words to start a baseball game. But I noticed as I looked down that he was still clinging to my wife rather standing next to the in-game host, Nate. As I looked even closer, it was Gideon who was standing there, prepared to shout into the microphone. Shiloh decided he did not want to do it, so big brother had to "pinch hit" for him.

Grandson pre-game prep.

Many years earlier there was another memorable time about the delivery of the ball and the resin bag. This little boy was probably around 5 or 6. As he was announced by the in-game host at the time, Rusty, he marched on his way to complete his mission. Never have I seen a child place the ball and resin bag down more carefully, almost to the degree of military precision, than this young boy. He was so proud of himself for doing what he was asked to do correctly. That baseball and resin bag were exactly where he placed them ... on 2nd base! He ran off the field beaming with confidence upon completing his task. Of course, no one had the heart to tell him of his "error." Once he left the field, Rusty went out and retrieved the items to place them on the mound.

Stepping out of the box: *Why is an injured player at times listed as day to day? Aren't we all day to day?*

2014 Season Poem (excerpt)
77-85 4th in AL East

Hannigan, Yates, Beliveau, Casali were all new
So was The Porch that gave the fans a unique view

2 seam and 4 seam fastballs are dependent on how you hold the stitches
Boxberger used both when he struck out the side with the bases loaded on 9 pitches.

Web-gems are a great defensive play as the game flows and ebbs
So if Alex makes a great play on the mound, is that a Cobb-Web?

The Outlaw came up in May and added a much-needed spark
Don't forget that he, Myers, and DeJesus hit homers that were inside the park

The Maddon Potato Head give-away not one but two
If it was up to me the byline should have read "Joe, this spud's for you."

The Forrest Gump of baseball, he saw it all and everyone liked him.
He was known as Skipper, Don, Popeye as we said goodbye to Zim.

Peanuts, Cracker Jacks... Nachos?

There are certain smells associated with baseball, like a hot dog being grilled, the enticing aroma of popcorn and the smell of fresh cut grass (*Wait I work in a dome*). Depending on the fan, the smells of the game can enhance their experience immensely. Let's be honest. Some people are more interested in the food than they are in the game. That is ok, it's part of the baseball tradition. After all, doesn't the "national anthem" of baseball have the lyrics "buy me some peanuts and cracker jacks?"

Speaking of that famous tune, it is one of the three most popular songs sung today, behind only *Happy Birthday and The National Anthem.*

As I mentioned above, one of the great smells of life that permeates through a ball park, among other places, is popcorn. It is as if those kernels popping have some type of hypnotic effect on us that is impossible to resist. (*Why is it when you go to the movies even after you just finished a meal, that smell draws you into buying some, even if you are not hungry?*) I remind fans as they come by me with their bag or bucket, headed back to their seats, that popcorn is one of the great smells of life. However, I also remind them that one of the worst smells is burnt popcorn! That smell just lingers, doesn't it?

"The love of popcorn is ageless!"

You might recall that I mentioned before that there are a significant number of steps, depending on your seat row, that you must go up and down during the game. (FYI in my section from the top down to the dugout is 51 steps-yep I counted.) Fans groan over the amount of steps and ask me, with a smile, when we are installing an escalator. I am quick to respond that I don't usually tell fans this but every inning we add another step. They look at me with a rather unsure smile. I then tell them that about the 6th inning when they have made numerous trips up and down they are going to believe me.

When fans come up the steps from a row further down, my comment is usually the following: "the good news is you are sitting close to the field, the bad news is you are sitting close to the field."

If people smile at my "witty" comment about proximity to the game, that leads me into the following discourse:

Sitting close to the field while walking up and down these steps means you can eat or drink whatever you want during the game. Obviously, you are going to walk the calories off. I then follow up with the following "dietary guidance." There are no calories when eating off someone else's plate since those calories were meant for the plate owner. Eating in front of the TV allows calories to be dissolved by the "radiation" coming from the television. Eating over the kitchen sink also nullifies calories as well. (Though it is not baseball season I have now started telling fans about NCD No Calories in December. Nothing you eat during the month has calories through New Years Eve.) I conclude by telling the fans that I am writing a diet book that will be totally worthless but it will be a bestseller.

Speaking of eats at the ballpark, I have noticed that one item continues to grow in popularity—ice cream. It seems to me that more and more people are enjoying this frozen treat regardless of the time of day or whether the game has started or not. Again, I have a comment for fans when they come by with their ice cream. I tell them that *you can never go wrong with ice cream ... it's just not for breakfast anymore!* Yep, a bit of a strange comment, but I have never had anyone disagree with me.

Speaking of food and the ballpark, it is there that you can witness what many say is impossible ... men multitasking. More than one time I have seen men eating a hotdog and drinking beer ... while walking!

Ahh beer, I guess you cannot have a baseball stadium book without mentioning the famous beverage. You would think someone who has been called *Bru* a few times would enjoy a *brew*, but that is not the case. I just can't get past the taste.

I have been offered more than once by a fan to buy me one during the game. (That would be a good look huh … me standing at the top of my section sipping on a brew while doing my job lol.) I admire the beer vendors that go up and down the steps hauling that traditional baseball beverage. Really, as I watch them trek around with that carrier of not only beers, but the ice which is melting and sloshing, my back tightens up. I cannot imagine the weight and stress that puts on their backs as they do it game after game. I have always found them to be friendly as well, as most of them are quite knowledgeable about the game. Obviously, they do not stand around long, as time is money, but it is hard to imagine a baseball game without them.

I do remember a beer vendor chanting through the stands … *De-hydration just say no … re-hydration just say yo!*

Then there was the day that I saw a young woman ordering cotton candy followed quickly by purchasing a beer! (Even as a non-beer drinker, immediately my lips started to pucker at that combination.) I guess I must have been staring, as she looked up and told me she did this all the time.

As is my style, even with beer drinkers coming back to their seats after purchasing their beverage, I have something to say. I remind them not to spill it going down the steps (honestly, that is partially selfish since if there is a spill, either I have to call for assistance, or if it is not as big a spill, then I clean it up myself). I tell the fans to "Save the Suds."

In my attempt at humor, I also remind them not to spill it in light of what it cost them to buy it. I ask them if they saw the loan officers out there to help them make their purchases. Also, if someone is returning to their seat and they are balancing a cup of beer in each hand (which I am assuming means one for someone else, though that can be an incorrect assumption), I tell them to sip out of each cup so as not to spill any. Some grin at what seems to them as to be a novel idea, while some others simply smile or wink and tell me they already have.

Another relatively new arrival to the ballpark fare is nachos. I know some of you are saying that you have been eating nachos for a long time at a baseball game, which is probably true. However, nachos have not been around as long, nor have they broken through the top 3 of popcorn, hot dogs, and peanuts.

It was during my first year working at The Trop that I had my initial encounter with nachos. I was filling in one game on the third base side and was standing at the top of the section. Batting practice was taking place and fans were beginning to make their way to their seats. I was facing the field when I heard a fan behind me say, "OH NO", as their food spilled onto the floor. Upon turning around, I saw that the man had dropped his entire order of nachos without ever taking even one chip. As a new Fan Host I wanted to assure him that this was not a problem. I would see to it that not only the mess would be cleaned up, but that he would also get a new order of nachos.

Being one of my first food encounters, I felt I was handling this situation rather calmly. It was then as I looked down again at the spilled mixture of cheese and chips that I noticed that the entire spill did not completely land on the floor behind me. Upon further inspection, there was no need for a replay review. I discovered a significant portion of the spill had landed on my khaki pants as well as my shoes. Yep, there were portions of chips and cheese dripping down my pants along with even more cheese baptizing my shoes. I took care of the poor fan who committed this "error," in getting him a new order, along with finding help to clean up the mess on the floor.

Then there came the reality of what I was going to do about myself. Remember, this happened during batting practice so the game had not even started yet. I cleaned myself up as much as possible, but there were numerous stains on my pants and a significant amount of cheese that was still oozing into my shoes and socks. As the game progressed so did my aroma. If anyone had thought the game had stunk, they needed to stand next to me for a half an inning and they would have changed their minds. It was quite an ordeal, but it would be the first of many times that I was *wearing* food while working. (See *Getting My Head in the Game chapter 10.*)

Stepping out of the box: *Why do we sing "Take Me Out to the Ball-game" when we are already there? (I know that is not an original thought but I still think about it.)*

2015 Season Poem (excerpt)
80-82 4th in AL East

Game after game went by and the continued outcome became surreal
It took Kevin Cash 11 games before he finally won a replay appeal.

To hit a game winning homer and be the winning pitcher sounds unthinkable ... garbage
Yet Nathan did that on the mound and at the plate as The Phillies experienced his Karn-age.

Stephen Souza Jr went on the DL being hit on the hand and broke a bone
I was wondering when he makes a call is his cell called a Souza Phone?

From the plate to the field, he was the heart and soul of the team in our glory days
It was only fitting that Carlos Pena came back to The Trop to retire with the Rays.

17 rookies got the call to The Show hoping to make it big and get rich
But what about Brandon Guyer who set a Rays record of 24 times getting hit by a pitch?

7

Fans

Baseball would not be The Great American Pastime, with fans worldwide, if it were not for those loyal supporters of their team who border on the fanatical. This of course is where we get the word "fan"! Greater than my love of the game, what makes me keep coming back season after season is the fun I have interacting with baseball fans. Note that I did not simply say Rays fans. The visiting team fans along with pure baseball fans who are not really rooting for either team also enhance my experience. At The Trop I intentionally go out of my way to make visiting team fans feel welcome. My goal is the same for any fans I come in contact with, that they will leave having a memorable experience regardless of the score. I am not always successful, but regardless, it is still my goal.

I probably interact with fans as much at the top of my sections as I do going down those infamous 51 steps. As I have said previously, I just finished my 16th season with The Rays. There are Fan Hosts who have been here even longer than me. At least three who have worked here the entire 26 years of the Rays. In addition to speaking at Rays U to the first year Fan Hosts, periodically I am asked to help train them onsite. During that time, I want to be thorough, and yet honest. For instance, I tell them if this was brain surgery we would not be talking. I am not the sharpest crayon in the box, but I would like to think I am one of the more colorful ones.

As I walk them through the basics, there is one thing I try to emphasize, which I believe is one of the most important. It is also one that I constantly am reminding myself numerous times each season. Body language plays a critical role for us as Fan Hosts. I need to regularly remind myself when I walk down those steps that most of the eyes of fans in my immediate sections, at least momentarily are on me. Regardless if I am going down for my usual half innings to the dugout, or to check on someone who might need assistance, the fans are watching. I might need to go down to address an issue that I have become aware of (profanity, vaping etc.) or I am headed down to tease a fan and joke with them. For whatever the reason, I am being watched. Therefore, my body language as well as my facial expressions are key. If the situation warrants, I might stand straight up and "look down" on the fan(s) to communicate the seriousness of the situation. Then there are times that I need to go down, but stooping to talk to someone is a much better non-confrontational approach.

There are also those fun moments which I pick up on and go down to laugh with a fan over what just occurred. For instance, if a fan drops a foul ball hit to them and it bounces away, I immediately head down to the fan. Once I determine that the only thing hurt is their pride, I tell them that I have to give them an "error" for misplaying that foul ball. I attempt to do a lot of fist bumping and smiling every game, regardless of what the scoreboard reads.

In all fairness to the fans, if you are not familiar with The Trop, returning to your section and seat can be confusing. On the 1st base side where I have worked now for the last 14 years, the top of the sections can all look the same. Even with my knowledge of The Trop, it still can be a challenge to help fans find their seats. Learning the unique way the rows are designed can initially be a head scratcher. Seat rows are lettered along with each seat being numbered starting from seat #1 to however many seats there are in the row going from home plate outward. The seats in my sections along the first baseline have 10 seats, which is not that challenging. However, when a person shows me their ticket, the seat number will determine which side of the row I send them down that is closest to where they are sitting.

When it comes to the lettered rows I mentioned a minute ago, that is quite a different challenge. The Trop is designed to have even numbered sections on the first base side and down right field, while the odd numbered sections are on the third base side and left field. In what seems to be a bit quirky, my fellow Fan Host Dennis reminded me it is just like addresses on a street. The odd number is one side while the even side is the opposite side of the street.

Now comes the challenge of the lettered rows! The very top row of the section farthest from the field is *JJ*. Yep, that is right double J, not A or even AA. From JJ the seat rows go backwards as you get closer to the field, so the next row is HH, followed by GG (there is no double I because II would be even more confusing), FF, and EE until you reach AA. Therefore row AA is 9 rows from the top of the section. Of course there are still more rows, next after AA comes Row Z. The rows continue to go backwards all the way down to Row K, which is the closest row to the field with the dugout immediately in front of your seat. (There also is no row O since that, too, would be too confusing. Stop smiling and shaking your head.) After working in my sections for all these years, I still am counting at times on my fingers so I can correctly tell the fan how far they need to go to reach their row.

As if the rows are not confusing enough, for some of our newer fans there can be even more questions. One evening a gentleman came in and showed me his ticket on his phone. I believe it was like section 116, row P and seat 8 was the third seat in. I instructed him that he was sitting down on the left; his seat was the third seat in and was 5 rows up from the dugout. To which he looked at me and seriously said, *"What's a dugout?"* That stunned me for a second upon never having been asked that before. I believe I walked him down to his seat to avoid any more confusion.

Numerous fans each game often wander back trying to find their seat or recognize someone that they are sitting next to. They might even be carrying food and drink which heightens their anxiety to return to locate where they came from. I often try to "study" people who are seated in my sections each game and identify them by something distinctive. Therefore, if they get "lost" I can "rescue" them if they are confused about what aisle to go down.

I must admit there are times when, before I can "rescue" one of my fans, I see them going down the wrong set of steps. They eventually discover their "error" at some part of their trek. When they finally return to where I am standing, and as they are preparing to proceed down the correct steps, I softly say to them while winking, *"You have nothing to worry about ... no one saw you go down the wrong section."*

To be fair to the fans, at times it can be confusing. There were a few years that their confusion had me baffled. For a couple of seasons there was an elderly couple who sat in the wheelchair seats at the very top of section 116. They were wonderful people to talk to and extremely loyal Rays fans. (I remember every game she stood up and sang out proudly the words to The National Anthem while her military veteran husband stood at attention and saluted.) Besides sitting at the top of the section each game, they each wore blue wigs in support of their Rays. They were a sight to see, cheering in those bright blue hairpieces. People would come by all the time and talk to them or take pictures of their distinctive look. During those years, I had a hard time wondering why the fans who sat in the section below them had trouble finding their seats when they returned. How could you forget, much less miss, these two bright blue beacons to remind you of your seat? Yet people still walked by them or looked aimlessly down the rows of seats to find their friends and family seated right in front of these two blue "lighthouses!"

I am a Rays fan as well as an employee, but I am also a fan of the game. Therefore, if you come to a game here at The Trop, hopefully you are looking forward to an experience that only the game of baseball can deliver. For all the seasons I have worked here, I am not sure there has been a game when I have not seen at least one fan wearing some type of Cubs gear. Regardless of who The Rays are playing, someone comes by at some point displaying their loyalty to their beloved Cubbies. Therefore, if a fan comes by me supporting a different team, I want them to know they are welcome, even if they do have poor taste in who they root for ... lol! I also try to say something regarding their team if something quickly comes to mind.

The combination of being a baseball fan, as well as interacting with visiting team fans, always comes to play the most for me when the Yankees are in town. Before you jump to conclusions, let me explain what I mean. The Yankees and their 27 world championships are very much a part of the history of the game. For all of you who might not like the Yankees, either past or present they are the pillar franchise. As a baseball fan (but not a Yankee fan), I recognize that. Almost without exception every Yankee game I work there comes a time when I get into a conversation with a "real" Yankee fan. Part of the Yankee tradition that they have upheld through all these years is that they have never put the players name on the back of their home or away jerseys. Did you know they were one of the first teams to put numbers on the back of their jerseys?

"In 1916, the Indians—responding to the complaints of scorekeepers, vendors and fans who couldn't tell who was who on the field—became the first team to experiment with uniform numbers, putting each player's lineup position on their sleeve. The experiment lasted only a few weeks before being shelved. The Cardinals tried something similar seven years later, only for the numbers to be scrapped due to what manager Branch Rickey called "continuing embarrassment to the players." Cut4 by MLB.com

The original numbers, at least for some of the Yankee greats, corresponded to what spot in the batting order they hit. (Hence Babe Ruth #3 since he hit third, Gehrig #4 etc.) When I see a Yankee fan come in wearing a jersey or t-shirt with the player's name, along with the number on the back ,it makes me *cringe* somewhat. That is not right baseball speaking. They should not be allowed to wear their #7 Mantle or #99 Judge shirt/jersey. Also, wherever they bought it should be banned as well. However, I just read that you can purchase a Yankees #4 Gehrig from the baseball Hall of Fame in Cooperstown! YIKES! I realize that this is my own issue and I should get over it but I haven't. Therefore, when I see a Yankee fan who has a historically accurate jersey on, I bring the whole topic up. Just about instantly we connect and a rapport takes place between us. Usually they are surprised that an "usher" would even talk to them, much less about a real Yankees issue. I have had fathers call their sons over to have me tell them my feelings, which of course reinforces what they have said. This is another way to enhance any fan's experience, which is not only my job, but my pleasure.

No name just #2-he even knows who wore #2 before Jeter!

Fans are the lifeblood of any sport and they enhance the game experience by their enthusiasm. We who call ourselves fans are a rare group, but we know that already don't we? *WE*, an interesting pronoun that fans use. Due to our loyalty, fans associate themselves with the team regardless of the outcome. WE lost today … WE didn't play well … WE hit the ball hard all game … WE made too many errors … you get the idea. As fans WE are a part of the team regardless if we have a jersey with a number/name on it or not.

There seems to be a lot of criticism of both professional and college sports these days, some of which might be justified. However, for all its flaws, sports provide something to our culture that is basically unique and needed—*community*. Sports unites geographical areas, bonds people together from diverse backgrounds, ethnicity, socio- economics, gender and age. Total strangers enter The Trop, but out of their loyalty for The Rays, in those next few hours they become "family" as they cheer and agonize together. After the game, depending on the result, they might leave out separate ends of the row and never cross paths again. But during those nine innings (or more), they develop a bond as fans, regardless if WE won or WE lost.

Each game I work, the dynamics of fans, for better or worse, is on display. I remember a mid-week afternoon playoff game where the atmosphere was electric. When I made my usual trek toward the dugout, to make sure everything was fine, there were some businessmen sitting a few rows from the field.

Some had their ties loosened having come straight from work. They all seemed to be having a good time. It was then, what I had interpreted as fan banter was becoming more escalated. Voices were being raised; accusations were being made as these men began shouting at each other. I realized quickly they were not joking around like I had originally thought. I began to see if I could get to the bottom of this commotion. As they continued in what seemed like more and more childish behavior, one man stood up and looked at me while pointing and said loud and clear , *"Well Bruce, he started it!"* I paused to process what he had just said, as did the fans around them. I looked at the fan that made that profound statement and said, *"Did you hear what you just said?"* I then reminded them of the price of these seats for a playoff game. I told them if they could not get their act together, security might need to come down here and settle this matter. Everything seemed to calm down after that. I went back up the steps thinking no one is going to believe me when I tell them what I just heard! (Oh yeah, speaking of fans, they were ALL cheering for The Rays!)

From my experiences at The Trop along with my own personal sports fan history, I have developed a theory of the *psychology of fans*. For our thinking, let's keep this to us as baseball fans.

Baseball fans cheer for players who don't know us.

For the most part baseball fans yell at players who can't hear us.

Baseball fans yell profound statements like ... get a hit or strike him out or catch the ball!

Baseball fans shout the exact same things at home in front of the TV!

For those non-baseball fans who make fun of us, remember those people are usually the ones, while watching a TV show or movie who say, *"Don't open that door." "Don't go down those steps"!*

At times we as fans can be fickle, can't we? We quickly have our perspective on pretty much everything in life tinted should our team win. Yet let our team lose and lose badly, and we just as quickly become devastated. I have often told my wife, I would rather The Rays lose big, *getting their doors blown off*, rather than by one run. In those one-run games, if one of any number of things, like a missed call, weather, (well not in The Trop), a bad bounce or lucky catch changed, then so could the outcome.

Fun at The Trop is contagious between Fans and Fan Hosts.

162 games (81 home games) is a lot of baseball, so that means I am going to watch a few "stinkers" throughout the season. For whatever the reason(s), The Rays did not play well that game. At times it is painful to watch. Every season there are few of those types of games that I work. Almost without fail the next game a fan or two will come up and say, "Bruce did you work last night's game? That was terrible, I had a hard time watching it at home." To which I reply, "yes, I worked that game, but you know the difference between me and you? *You could change the channel.*"

Fans are not only fickle, but they are also funny. Whether intentional or not, they add to my enjoyment of doing my job. *Usually, the more insistent a fan is about knowing where their seat is, the more wrong they are.* I told a fan one day that his seat was 5 rows down (EE) on the left and four seats in (7). He kind of blew me off (not the first time) and said he knew where he was going. Well, he went way down past the 5 rows and then he looked left and then right. He came back up a few rows but still could not find that seat that he "knew." This went on for a bit before I went down to help. As I approached him, I noticed what was printed on his T-shirt, "MENSA"! (Maybe one of his smart friends bought him the shirt.)

When games go to extra innings, a different dynamic emerges within The Trop with both Fan Hosts and fans. As you can imagine, they can be long and tiring. My time at The Trop precedes MLB's decision in extra innings to start with a runner on 2nd base. Certainly, that has increased the possibility of games ending sooner. That is probably good for the fan, as well as the players, along with the media coverage. (Let the record show that none of the Fan Hosts would disagree either.) However, before that rule was put into place, there were endless games that seemed that seemed to go on forever. I think with some fans there comes a place in an extra innings game that says I have stayed this long. I might as well stay to see how this game ends.

From 2012-2017 the Rays had a pitcher on their roster named Jake Odorizzi (Odor-izzy) who pitched well for us (*US the fan pronoun strikes again*). When those extra-inning games dragged on after a while, I needed something to say to the fans who were still here. During the half innings I would begin walking up to fans and say the concession stands were now serving breakfast. How do you want your eggs? I would ask and then quickly respond "Odorizzi?" When people did not immediately smile, but gave me that glassy eye look, it was then I realized that the yolk was on me. (*Shameful right ... hey look on the bright side. At least you're not married to me!*)

Sometimes fans want to offer me advice.

Throughout the season we get fans from other parts of the world here on vacation (holiday). They at times need assistance and I am happy to help them in any way I can. For most of them, this is the first time they have seen a baseball game, so they have lots of questions. I remember talking with a family here from the UK. During our conversation the father kindly said that baseball was very hard to understand. I smiled and said perhaps he was right, but could he explain cricket to me. He paused, started to say something, and then smiled and said, "good point."

Often as a Fan Host, I get asked any number of questions, which are to be expected. One time a fan asked me if there was any way I could get him a toothpick. That one had me stymied for a while, first by the request, and then was it even possible to find one. With some assistance from Guest Services (they have helped me on more than one occasion) and some searching on my own, I located a toothpick for the fan. I came back feeling pretty good about being able to find what I thought was probably a lost cause.

Now, in doing my job, I have always said, if you like people and baseball you will do just fine. However, for me it also requires the ability to read people, and rather quickly. This definitely holds true with my sense of humor. Usually more than once a game, I get the same understandable question. Fans coming up the steps from their seats will ask where is the closest restroom? This is now where my humor radar has to kick in immediately. If I feel they have a low *"fun quotient,"* I simply point them in the right direction, which is not too far from the top of the section. If however, my radar tells me that they enjoy some nonsense, my response changes. When asked where the closest restroom is, I look them straight in the eyes, and with a serious tone say, *"Oh I am sorry we had to close them for COVID and they are still not open."* I get any number of looks and smiles, but there was one response I will never forget. A woman looked at me and winked as she said, never tell a pregnant woman that!-NOTED!

Speaking of fun with fans, we as Fan Hosts are often asked to take pictures of people while at the game. Since we have done it so much, we might even suggest a different angle or location, depending on the lighting or the site line. When I take pictures for fans, again my humor radar kicks in. If the radar tells me that these fans will appreciate it, while taking their picture I will also take a selfie or two without them knowing it. Most of the time I do not tell them and wait for them to look at the pictures, or maybe they are surprised once they get home to see my smiling face. (I am sure the delete feature is used often.)

During the middle of the 2nd, 4th, 6th, 7th and 8th innings, I am required to go down to the dugout and turn around with my back to the field and face the fans. This serves many purposes, including making me visible, as well as "guarding" the dugout (so people do not climb on it for any reason). Oftentimes this gives me the opportunity to talk with the fans about any number of topics, which I enjoy. Of course, during this break in the action there is usually something going on the Jumbotron.

Many times when I am down there, the *Dippin' Dots* shuffle is going on. That consists of either Rays hats or devil rays with a ball under one of them. The hats or rays are moved around (*think a shell game—wait can I say that?*) while a child who has been selected is trying to figure out which hat/devil ray the ball is under when the shuffling stops. While standing down at the dugout as this is going on, I so enjoy watching people glued to that Jumbotron screen as if National Security is at stake. Once the shuffling has stopped, they immediately shoot up their hand indicating with their fingers which is the correct answer. I will admit, most of the time they are right. I will then go up to them and smile as I congratulate them on their skills of observation.

Now the challenge in finding the right hat/ray is nothing compared to the one the in-game host may have with the child. Most of the time the child makes the right selection, but the fun begins when there is a child insisting on guessing the wrong hat/ray. Believe it or not, there are some strong-willed children who come to baseball games. Trying to convince them to guess again (and maybe again) until they get it right can become quite challenging. Remember, this is during the half inning of the game. Somehow I do not think the umpire will stop the pitch clock for *Dippin' Dots*. The pressure is really on the in-game host, presently Nate, because you cannot tell a child they do not get ice cream in front of thousands of fans. That is a bad resume builder.

Speaking of the Jumbotron, it is fascinating how fans react when they see themselves up on the giant screen. I have seen some amazing reactions and extreme behavior by kids and adults alike. Through the years, my theory is that the more extreme the behavior of an adult fan on the screen, the more conservative their job is during the week. Just a theory...

For a few seasons I had a fan sitting up in the wheelchair row right next to me in seat 1. He was an enthusiastic and knowledgeable fan. We would often talk about baseball, especially what we thought the Rays should or should not do on the field. Steve was a great fan who really got into the game.

Some years back, when Ozzie Timmons was the Rays first base coach (a real fan favorite), he had an unusual tradition. At the end of an inning, when the Rays scored, Ozzie would do 10 pushups for each run. It became quite a spectacle in the dugout for the players and the fans who got to see it. Well, Steve loved this idea so much he had a poster made that was probably 10 feet long. The sign with white letters on a blue background, read, MAKE OZZIE DO PUSH UPS. He would unroll it each game he came to and tape it on the railing in front of the wheelchair seats. Before one game, he asked me to take his picture standing behind the sign. I had him send the picture to me; it is a great reminder of a loyal Rays fan.

The late "Wild Pitch" Steve.

More than that, though Steve was known for his unique and un-timely cheer. When The Rays were batting, regardless at times of who was or was not on base, he would yell, WILD PITCH! He said it so loudly and often that it became a joke around the area. We would even refer to him as *Wild Pitch*. Finally, the joke was on us. The Rays had a runner on third, and as the pitch left the pitcher's hand, Steve yelled his famous *Wild Pitch* chant. At that moment, the pitch sailed past the catcher to the screen and The Rays scored, to the delight of all of us. Honestly, I am not sure if we cheered more for the Rays scoring or for our friend "Wild Pitch" Steve.

Fans at the game, besides interacting with food and beverage vendors, also encounter the 50/50 sellers. These enthusiastic vendors are providing fans the opportunity to purchase tickets to potentially split the pot of the money collected. Toward the end of the game, the winning ticket used to be displayed on the scoreboards. If you won, you received your "50," with the other half going to The Rays Baseball Fund, a charity which does great work within the Tampa Bay Community. (Note: now the winning number is not displayed on the scoreboard but can be found on the QR code printed on your ticket at the end of the game.) Potentially this allows the fans to win an even larger amount right up to the last out.

With the 50/50 you can win at the game regardless of the score!

At times, fans will ask me what happens if they have the winning ticket. I calmly tell them to just *give it to me and I will take care of it for them. If they seem skeptical, I tell them that I will settle for 7%.*

On more than one occasion, I have known fans sitting in or near my sections have won. Honestly, I had a couple who won twice during the same home stand. (Pretty amazing huh?)

One evening about 5 years ago, there was a husband and wife who were sitting in the *Rays Club*, now known as *The Baldwin Club*, which is an area that includes all you can eat and drink. Those club seats extend along the first base line directly behind the sections where I am positioned. Late in the game they flagged me down wondering if I had seen any of the 50/50 vendors. The couple wanted to buy tickets and time was running out before they stopped selling them. *(Now sales do not stop until the end of the game.)* I spotted a vendor who came over to this couple and the transaction took place. Honestly, I have no idea how many tickets they had purchased as once they met up with the vendor I walked away.

I would say it was about an inning later that the winning ticket was announced and displayed. Yep, you guessed it, they had won. Obviously, they were ecstatic, so I walked over to them to offer my congratulations and to see how much "we" had won.

Since they were seated in the club level, they had to go over to the Gate 4 elevator and come down to Gate 3 to claim their prize at Guest Services. I explained all that to them, as the husband got up to proceed to the elevator. It was then that I told him that I would walk over to Guest Services, which is not far from where I work, and let them know he was coming with the winning ticket. Upon arriving at Guest Services and telling them the winner was on his way, the husband arrived and of course he was very excited. I then walked back to my section where his wife was still sitting alone in her seat. As I approached her, I let her know that I ran into her husband claiming their winning ticket. I then went on to say that he was paid in cash and that he told me to tell her he would send her a postcard! For about three seconds she freaked out! With a smile on my face, I told her there was no way they would ever pay him in cash, which made her calm down. I walked away with a smile on my face knowing I got the reaction I was hoping for.

"The enthusiastic 50/50 vendors are in *A League of Their Own*."

Some of my favorite fans are the kids. There is something special about seeing the game of baseball through their eyes. Many come to celebrate a special occasion, like the end of school or their birthday. When we know about it, we try to make a child's birthday a big deal. As Fan Hosts, we will go and get them a birthday badge that they can wear proudly on their special day at The Trop. There is a place on the badge for their name to be written so it can be personalized. Normally with kids, once I realize it is their birthday, I will ask them how old they are. This is followed up by the question, are *you married*? Upon the expected NO answer, I then ask if they have a girl or boyfriend. This tends to get some interesting looks and even responses.

One Sunday afternoon game I was helping with the pre-game autographs for kids. There, in line was Antonio, who I knew from other games, along with his mom. I had not seen them for awhile, but I knew that his mom was expecting. As he was standing in line, I noticed his birthday badge and said, "Happy Birthday Antonio!" I asked him if he was married, and he politely shook his head, no. My follow-up girlfriend question received a soft innocent, *No, I have a baby sister!*

Here's to our boomerang fans who keep coming back!

Some of my favorite people are those fans who return year after year regardless of how the previous season ended. Their return makes my job even more enjoyable. Many of them I stay in contact with during the off-season.

My thanks go to those fans who brave the air conditioning each game.

(Seriously, it can get chilly in The Trop, sometimes especially in the sections I work. The fans there probably have more sweatshirts/hoodies brought or bought at the team store than anywhere else in the Dome.)

Here's to those non fair-weather fans.

They are here regardless if there is a deluge outside The Trop. Remember in a domed stadium we play regardless of the weather, where other games would be rained out.

There was a game some years ago during the 2013 season when I saw a strange occurrence in the seats. A father and his two adult age children were switching seats. *They were NOT trying to move closer to the field but farther away!* Obviously, this caught my attention so I had to go down and ask what was going on. As

I approached them, the father, Dominick immediately began to explain the situation. He was from New York (hated the Yankees), but was a long time Mets fan until the Bernie Madoff association with the Mets ownership. As an avid baseball fan, he was intrigued by The Rays and how they remained competitive year after year in the AL East. He showed me his Rays wristwatch as a sign of his loyalty. That evening, his children were attending their first major league game. At one point Dom realized his seats were too close to the field for them to truly appreciate the beauty and complexity of the game, so he wanted to move back a few rows for a better view. (If you are wondering if this was the only time I have had fans move further away, I would pretty much say, yes, with a few extenuating circumstances involved.)

This unique encounter has led me to a true baseball friendship that has extended beyond that night at The Trop. Dom, still lives in NY, yet faithfully follows the Rays like no one I know. He works for the MLB Network behind the scenes. He regularly makes sure that the on-camera hosts are acutely aware of what is going on in St. Petersburg with his beloved Rays. He is not only an avid fan, but well educated. As each new season unfolds, I am on the lookout at the team stores for when the current media guide arrives, so that I can send him one. He reads that guide from cover to cover and is well-versed in player stats and regularly texts me when a player has reached a significant milestone in Rays team history. This is another example of what makes fans so special and unpredictable. Here I make contact with a "New Yorker" who is switching seats and find out he is one of the most diehard Rays fans I have ever met.

I really want fans, and especially the ones I come in contact with, to enjoy their experience at the game, regardless of the score. It hit me during the middle of the 2022 season of perhaps another way to add to the fun at The Trop. While watching both professional and college baseball, there was a trend taking place in the dugout after a teammate had hit a homerun. Teams had created their own unique celebration, like having the *homer hitter* wear a particular piece of clothing or carry a significant object once they returned to the dugout. (White Sox—mobster coat; Nationals—powdered wig; Twins—fishing vest; Angels—Samurai Warrior helmet; Mariners—Trident). Everyone involved seemed to be having fun, after all baseball is a game!

I began to think about what I could provide for the fans sitting in my sections to celebrate a Rays home run. There were obviously some restrictions like time, since the game continued after the homer. It had to be quickly accessible, along with fun. Then whatever "celebration" happened, it must be noticeable by at least some of the fans in the sections. I quickly ruled out jumping up on the dugout and running around like a mad man. Mainly, because I am not sure how long it would take me to get up on the dugout (if it took me to the next inning somehow the moment would have been lost), and I wanted to keep my job. FYI—no one is allowed up on the dugout except The Ray Team ("cheerleaders" who are some of my favorite people in the Trop), along with Raymond and DJ Kitty—the team mascots! No, this homer hoopla had to be fun for and directly impact the fans. (I didn't think my bosses would approve of me buying everyone a beer. Besides it would bust my non-existing budget).

No one works harder but has more fun than The Ray Team.

Like other teams' celebrations, I thought it could be some kind of clothing that a fan could put on once a Rays player homered. Then it hit me—this seemed quite practical and met all of my concerns regarding the limitations. Surely someone had thought of this idea before, but I had never heard of it being done. *This idea was so good, I told my wife it was genius. She questioned me, genius?*

Right after the All-Star break in 2022, I introduced the *Home Run Derby!* Yep, an actual Derby hat that a fan could wear once a Rays player went deep. I bought a reasonably priced navy blue Derby. Then, my daughter, Amanda and wife, using a "cricut" (a computerized vinyl cutting machine), created a light blue script heading adhered to the front of the hat that read "Home Run Derby". On the back was the Rays yellow burst image. I have the Derby up at the top of the section aisle next to me in a bag.

As soon as I know a ball is gone, and often before it even hits the seats, I grab the Derby and I am off down those steps. To be honest, as fans arrive in my sections, I am scouring them for possible D*erby wearers*. I am looking for someone who is enthusiastically celebrating and wearing Rays gear. In the past two-

and-a-half years of celebrating I have had men, women, children, and senior fans wear the Derby. Everyone seems to look good in a Derby and no one has refused me.

The Derby looks great on fans of all ages!

As the player is circling the bases, I am explaining to the fan what is going on and why. They immediately put it on and wear it proudly. Often the friends or family they have come with start taking pictures of them wearing the hat. *Normally* they get to wear the Home Run Derby until the end of the inning. I then come down with a picture of some of the Rays players celebrating a homerun to give to them in exchange for the Derby. On the back of the picture, I have placed a sticker that says:

I wore the HOME RUN DERBY on (I write the date of the game).

THANKS TO: (I also write the name of the player who hit the homer).

It makes a nice memento of the game and the experience the fan had. I then exchange the Derby for the picture, which of course assures me I get my Derby back. (Before putting the Derby back in the bag, I have a small aerosol can of Lysol that I spray in the inside of the hat, in case you were worried that I forgot about hygiene.)

The very first fan to wear The Home Run Derby.

Now, I did say *normally* the fan gets to wear the derby until the end of the inning, but there are a couple of exceptions. If, for instance, the homer is hit with two outs in the inning and the next batter makes an out, then I let the fan wear the hat through the top of the next inning. A few times it gets to be a bit of a challenge when The Rays hit more than one homerun in an inning. It has happened-a few times there are *back- to-back jacks,* then I am running up and down the aisles like a crazy guy realizing that

I am not as young as I used to be. If the fan has to give the Derby up after a short time on their head, they seem to understand. Receiving the picture does "ease their pain" a bit. All in all, everyone seems to have a good time especially knowing the reason for the whole thing is that the Rays have hit a homer.

I had a big Rays fan during the 2023 season who recently had moved here from the UK. He was thrilled to wear the Derby once I explained the significance. From atop of the section, I even saw him stand up and pose for his wife with the Derby in place. When I eventually returned to retrieve the hat along with the picture, he "needed" a moment. It was then that he wanted his wife to take another photo of him, still wearing the Home Run Derby and holding the picture. Finally, he then went one step further and asked me to be in the picture with him, which of course I agreed. (I had them forward me a copy; it really is a fun picture). Moments like that are special for me and I am thrilled to be able to provide even more fun at the game.

There is one time a fan does not get to wear the Home Run Derby. One of my responsibilities is to be at the dugout once the game ends. Therefore, if the batter at the plate can end the game, I make sure I am down there. If a walk-off homer occurs, I stand up and cheer with everyone else and place the Derby on top of my Rays hat, kind of a "doubleheader."

Always smiles after a Rays victory!

Stepping out of the box: *Why do people who try to sneak into a seat choose to sit on the aisle?*

2016 Season Poem (excerpt)
68-94 5th in AL East

In spring training guys work on their golf game, fish and even scuba
This spring The Rays went with the President to play in Cuba.

Last season he became our regular at 2b, he plays the game hard and right.
By signing him to a multi-year extension, The Rays showed some Forsythe!

A come from behind win early on showed the team's ability to Rays-Up.
On that first $2 hot dog day, the comeback showed that The Rays knew how to ketchup!

One game Jake Odorizzi pitched his heart out with his splitter.
Yet amazing enough he lost to The Yankees on a one hitter!

We would all agree that with the year he had our MVP was Lon-go.
We also all came together as a sell-out crowd to declare *We Are Orlando!*

My Dome Away From Home

Tropicana Field has been my baseball home for 26 years. As I mentioned previously, I was coming to games as a fan for 10 years before I became a Fan Host. The Trop gets a bad rap from an assortment of people, many of whom have never set foot in the building. I have lost count of the number of first-time fans, including visiting team fans, who say, *this place is great; what's wrong with playing here?* Like any other stadium, it has its quirks, but there sure is a lot to love about our Trop.

Beginning with that, The Trop is a dome, not a retractable roof stadium-the only one in Major League Baseball. When new fans arrive, they ask about the roof and are often surprised that it is permanent. Does it prevent the Florida sunshine from coming in? Yes! Does it also keep us from having to deal with the high Florida temperatures and oppressive humidity? Yep! We enjoy, or should I say we are *spoiled*, watching Rays baseball with air conditioning at a pleasant 72 degrees. Besides keeping out the Florida heat and humidity, it also protects us all from the frequent afternoon or evening thunderstorms which can come quickly. and at times are lengthy. As you hear that thunder booming and lightning crashing outside The Trop, you can continue to watch the game uninterrupted.

We have never had a game rained out that I can remember, but we have had a few "rain delays." In my early days working, I do recall having power outages when lightning (not the hockey team) struck in the area. At times, the lights would flicker. Then other times, we did have power outages that temporarily knocked out some of the lights. During those times, we, as Fan Hosts working in the bowl, would walk down to the dugout to calm people's concerns. There were backup generators that would keep the electricity running to some degree. However, it would take some time for the field lights to come back on. During those days of diminished light, Bugs Bunny baseball cartoons were shown on the Jumbotron. Really, when you think about it, this all makes sense, since (baseball) *diamonds have carats and rabbits like carrots!*

Speaking of games, the facility which has been known as Tropicana Field since 1996 (originally named the Florida Suncoast Dome, then the Thunder Dome in 1993), has hosted many significant sporting events, as well as some big-name concerts.

Through the years you could have attended concerts featuring *Eric Clapton, David Bowie. AC/DC, Billy Joel, Guns N' Roses, Rod Stewart and KISS.* The Rays began offering post-game concerts in 2007 (*Sha Na Na*) featuring a variety of genres to appeal to an assortment of fans. After enjoying Rays baseball on certain games, you may have stayed and listened to the music of *The Beach Boys, LL Cool J, ZZ Top, Kenny Loggins, The Village People, Joan Jett and REO Speedwagon.* Even this past season of 2024, we had the music of *Jimmy Eat World, Riley Green and T-Pain.* To be perfectly honest, those concerts after a game can get long! Especially if I don't know the music. As I get older, the music seems to be getting louder. (Hmm is there a correlation?)

Overall, The Rays have been quite successful on concert nights— if my math is correct I think their winning percentage is around .630.

Prepping for the post game Village People concert.

But our beloved Trop has hosted more than baseball and concerts.

- **NBA** exhibition game with the Bulls (Jordan/Pippen)-**1990**
- **NCAA**-various rounds of the men's tournament including the Final Four-**1999**
- **NHL**-Lightning played here, including Stanley Cup playoffs-**1996**
- **Arena Football**- *The Tampa Bay Storm* including Arena Bowl IX-**1995**
- **NCAA Bowl Games**-including East/West Shrine game
- **United Football League**-**2009** (*Go Florida Tuskers*)
- **WTA** Davis Cup 3-day event-**1990**
- **Motor Sports**-*Sprint* Cars race-parking lot-**1992**
- **WWE-Professional Wrestling** including Royal Rumble-**2024** *48,044 Trop attendance record*

Anticipating "Royal Rumble."

Then there is **MLB**
- 1st game March **(3/31/98)**
- Site of Wade Boggs 3000 hit **(8/7/99)**
- 1st game that used instant replay (**9/3/08**)
- 1st game when replay overturned the call on the field (**9/19/08**)
- **2008** World Series
- **2013** Relocated game from Baltimore due to social unrest, where The Rays were the visiting team
- **2017** Relocated Houston home series due to flooding from Hurricane Harvey in which The Rays did not play

I am not sure there is any stadium, dome or other arena in America which can list all the above on "their resume."

Did you know that the infield dirt at The Trop must be watered 365 days a year? Not far below the surface is concrete, so if the dirt is not watered each day, it will begin to crack. Therefore, regardless of the weather (storms) or the calendar (holidays), someone from the Grounds Crew is there every day to be sure the watering takes place.

The Trop has its own unique baseball flavor. There is the rotunda, as you enter, which is modeled after the one at Ebbets Field in Brooklyn years ago. Then there is the orange glow of its famous dome after a Rays victory.

A Rays victory followed by a concert.

For a while, a touch of nostalgia was added with an organ being played during the game. The organ was originally not seen by the fans, but was then moved out to above center field. Of course, that relocation was an *organ transplant.*

Often the thing that bothers most critics of The Trop are the catwalks. These are part of the dome's support structure. The four rings that encircle the field have periodically come into play when a ball strikes one of them. Each ring has its own unique ground rules. Then, there are the times when what goes up does not come down. That means I have seen both fair and foul balls head up to the catwalks, but never to return. They are lodged up there. *If you have ever wondered the fate of those "lost baseballs," I have an answer for you.*

There is a gentleman named Larry, who along with his wife, Sharon, are season ticket holders that sit in my section. I found out that he was the Project Superintendent for the installation of the fabric roof for The Trop. Periodically throughout the season, he makes his way up to the catwalks to retrieve those "lost" baseballs. I have seen him on many occasions come to a game with multiple baseballs in his backpack. During the game, he will go over to a child and hand them one. There is something about being a baseball fan and getting an official ball at the game that makes this sport unique. Then, when a child receives one totally unexpected, their smile is contagious.

Larry shared with me the following story. Back before they put up the netting by the dugout, the kids would run down the aisle when The Rays were returning from the field, in hopes of getting a baseball thrown to them. One night, sitting about four rows in front of him and Sharon was a young boy, about 7 or 8 with his mother. Every inning he would run down in hopes of getting a ball, but no luck, since the taller kids had the advantage.

About the 7th inning, Larry went down to the young discouraged fan and asked to see his glove. He was somewhat reluctant, but he handed it over to Larry, at which time he stuck a ball into it. The boy was so excited and thanked him repeatedly. This young boy was a "real" Rays fan, as he was wearing a Rays t-shirt, hat and socks. As Larry returned to his seat, his mother turned around to say thanks, as well.

The next inning, the boy ran down the aisle, and as luck would have it, he got a ball! Upon returning to his seat and sitting down, he now had something to think about. With a ball in each hand, he was looking back and forth from one ball to another.

Then, without any prompting from his mother, this young boy got up from his seat. He walked down a few rows and gave one of the balls to a couple who had about a 3-year- old son. Larry began to tear up as he looked down at his chest, pounding with pride and hope for the future. Once the young Rays fan returned to his seat, Larry walked down and shook his hand and told him if he carried that attitude through life, he would be successful.

In one of my conversations with Larry at a game, I asked him what it is like to go up to those famous catwalks. He then off-handedly said to me, *"Bruce if you ever want to go up there sometime, let me know."* I was quick to take him up on his offer, thinking I will never get this offer or opportunity again. So, during the offseason both, my wife, Jeanette and I met Larry at The Trop and we ascended to those catwalks. It was truly an amazing experience that I will not forget. Is it high? Yep! I think all the way to the top is about 240 feet. But also, once you are up there, it really is a series of steps and railings. We took some great pictures of that unique view. Oh yeah, in case you were wondering I did not see even one feline up there. Hmm it makes you wonder if DJ Kitty has even been up on those catwalks?

From the Top of The Trop.

Speaking of DJ Kitty, a female fan came up to me during one game and was a bit concerned. She said "I think DJ Kitty is checking me out." I replied that she did not have anything to worry about, that it was simply a *"Cat-scan."* (*I made this story up, but I love to tell it to fans, to see their reaction.*)

Did you know that in 2012, in conjunction with the Republican National Convention held in Tampa Bay, a Kickoff Party was held at The Trop? Besides the uniqueness of the event, it was the only time Fan Hosts were off on a Sunday during a home stand.

When you consider all that The Trop hosts, there really isn't an *off season*. There are, or have been graduations, gymnastic meets, band competitions, banquets, home shows, and the last few years hosting *Enchant*, a Christmas extravaganza. Which means there really are very few days that The Trop is *Dome Alone*!

Stepping out of the box: *How has the Wave survived this long?*

2017 Season Poem (excerpt)
80-82 3rd in AL East

New turf was installed this year to make sure of no bad hops
But when the Rays traded Mahtook was that the ultimate Mike-drop?

There was a time in the season when the pitching staff just seemed stuck
Then came Jake Faria to the rescue along with his rubber duck!

In Houston, Longo hit for the cycle which everyone liked
For his cycle wouldn't it have been cool if The Rays would have given him a bike?

Souza gave fans in Minnesota a chuckle in their seats
When he dove for a ball that he missed by 30 feet!

Longo won another Gold Glove which we were all happy to see.
It seemed only appropriate that for Evan that Golden Glove was #3.

Foul Balls

Foul balls play a unique role in baseball in that they connect the fans with the players in an odd sort of way. Once a ball enters the stands, I have seen an assortment of behavior entail. At times it can be comical, but of course, there is a danger associated with it as well. I read about a woman (not at The Trop) who had her nose broken by a foul ball. Then on the next pitch, another foul ball hit her and broke her leg! That is why I was glad when MLB instituted having protective netting installed in stadiums behind the dugout and down the foul lines.

I understood the complaints by some of the season ticket holders who had seats near the dugout and felt their sight lines to the game were a bit distorted. However, there are many people who sit close to the field who are not paying attention to every pitch. A foul ball can come back quickly, with no warning. *Foul balls are not on a schedule where you can look at your watch and be prepared for that 7:45 ball coming your way.* Honestly, you can be attentive to the action and a foul ball can still hit you.

At the top of each section, at least foul pole to foul pole, is ADA (American Disabilities Act) or wheelchair seating. The tickets can be purchased by people who either come by wheelchair or are brought to their seats by Fan Hosts that are called *Rolling Rays*. They bring fans who ask for wheelchair assistance to their seats. Now, these seats are not exclusively for these fans, but they are available for those who choose to purchase them. These cushioned chairs are individually numbered for those who have a ticket. Some people sit in their wheelchairs during the game, so we remove the chair from the area.

It was in 2009, I believe, I was again working down the first base line beyond the bag. During the game, one of our fans and I were having an enjoyable chat about baseball among other things as she sat in her wheelchair. At one point, as we were talking and watching the game, Jason Bartlett (yea, I remembered the player, maybe because he was one of my favorite Rays at the time) hit a screaming line drive foul ball in our direction. This was before the screening was placed above the dugout and down the foul lines. The ball was hit so hard you could hear it "humming." We both saw it at the same time and instinctively turned in opposite directions away from this "screamer" foul ball. The ball directly hit and broke the cup holder in front of her seat, exploding her drink up in the air with soda and ice showering all over. I turned back to her immediately to see if she was ok. She was dripping in soda and ice. At first she said nothing. During her pause she began to move her arms next to her sides, Then, without saying a word, but with a smile as big as a child on Christmas morning, she held up the ball. It had wedged between her and her wheelchair. Other than being saturated, she could not have been happier. We shared a huge laugh together, along with a great sigh of relief that she was not hurt. She also had an unforgettable souvenir.

Between the first and second level where I work, there are three-dimensional thick plastic letters protruding from the façade that identify the name of the club level seating. During a Yankee game some years ago, Derek Jeter was batting. He fouled off a pitch that hit one of those plastic letters. The ball remained lodged inside the letter, but some jagged pieces of that thick plastic fell to the ground around me and the fans. Immediately my lead, Bill Shane, and I quickly picked those pieces up once we were sure that no one was injured. While we were picking up those shards of plastic, we were barraged by Yankee fans wanting a piece. We quickly told them they could not have any of it for what we thought were obvious reasons. They countered that we did not understand, they needed a piece of that plastic because Jeter had hit the ball that broke it. We then explained that under no circumstances, regardless who hit the ball, were we going to be giving out shards of plastic to fans. (I just recently found out that Bill was even offered money for a piece of "Jeter memorabilia"!)

 A few seasons ago, I had a female fan sitting with friends in row HH, seat 9. That is the second row from the top and the second seat from the aisle. To put it mildly, she was terrified of foul balls. Putting this in context, this was after the screens had been installed behind the dugout. Now to be *fair,* regarding a foul ball (*I'm hopeless*), the screen only prevents most of those screaming line drives, unlike my soda-soaked wheelchair fan. There are those high pop fouls that can land anywhere.

Regardless where a foul ball headed that night, this fan prepared herself. The moment she heard the crack of the bat and saw the ball was not in play, she "got into position." Her defensive posture was to immediately place her hands over her head, palms up, and squatted down in front of her seat. Please understand this was her *default position,* regardless where the foul ball was headed. So even if she was sitting here on first base up from the dugout and a foul ball was headed over to the visiting team bullpen past third base, she still put her hands over her head. To be honest, it was getting to be comical after a while, but that was what she chose to do. Then it happened! About the seventh inning, a high foul ball went over our heads into the 300 level. She, of course, immediately went into her protective crouch. This particular foul ball bounced out and came back down into the lower section as they sometimes do. The difference with this foul ball is that it came directly down and landed into the palms of this lady's hands, who blindly caught it. Not only did the ball come right to her, but without flinching or knowing what was about to happen, she snagged that foul ball. It was amazing to see what was an almost impossible catch. I am not sure I would have believed it if I had not seen it myself. Upon making the catch, but before she brought the ball down from her hands over her head, her eyes got as big as baseballs as she began to realize what had just happened! Obviously, there was quite a bit of commotion among her friends, as well as the fans around her. For those few moments, no one in the immediate area was paying attention to the game. Of course, to all who were on the field, from players to the umpires, this was just another foul ball that entered the stands. Once the excitement quieted down a bit, I wanted to go over to her and say, if there ever was a day for you to play the lottery, this is obviously your day. I simply thought it to myself as she continued to squeeze her treasure ever so tightly.

For us as Fan Hosts, when a foul ball lands in our sections, we are to immediately go down to be sure no one is hurt, which is usually the case. Honestly, most of the time the only thing hurt is the fan's pride for not catching the ball. Rarely does the first person who touches the ball catch it. Which leads to two observations from one who has seen a ton of foul balls enter the stands.

First, if you end up getting a foul ball as the result of it bouncing around, or it rolled under your seat, don't hold it up and show everyone like you accomplished a great fete. You just picked a ball up dude!

Secondly, I realize there are some rare exceptions, but for the most part adults who bring their gloves to the game are not very good. I have lost count how many "errors" I have seen adults make in trying to catch a foul ball with their glove. Honestly, at times it gets embarrassing. While the kids with gloves are *flash-ing leather* when foul balls come their way, adults are usually fumbling or have the ball hit their glove and bounce out. I just want to say to that adult, "Sir, you were not very good in little league 30 years ago and nothing has changed. Leave your glove in the trunk of your car."

Speaking of adults with gloves, there are some exceptions. I be-came acquainted with Irv years ago on Sunday afternoon games. He had two tickets right on the field down the first base line. Most games he sat there with his granddaughter. He brought his glove and I noticed he often had an assortment of baseballs. Even though he was not sitting in my section, I would often sit be-hind him when a seat was available in the 9th inning of the game while waiting to go on the field for the kids to run the bases. We would often talk about baseball and The Rays, but I noticed a number of players and coaches would acknowledge him as they walked by. This got my curiosity up to ask him about the recogni-tion, as well as the baseballs.

I found out that Irv had been a season ticket holder since the early 2000's. He loved his seats down there right by the field since he was able to interact with the players as they warmed up, stretched, and threw near him. His whole family were huge sports fans, so this up close and personal view was a dream come true. He brought his 50+ year-old Rawlings Brooks Robin-son model glove (childhood flashback) to catch foul balls in that area. As Irv would converse with the players, he let them know that his youngest daughter worked on staff at a local hospital as a member of the Psychiatry Team. Her duties took her to every floor in seeing patients of all ages, many who were there for long-term treatment.

Irv would ask the players to sign the balls that he caught or had been tossed to him so that his daughter could give them away to patients at the hospital. Most of them were pediatric patients who were undergoing a variety of illnesses. Upon hearing his story, an assortment of players and coaches like Ben Zobrist, Joey Wendle, Kevin Kiermaier and bullpen coach Stan Boroski would readily sign. The balls served as rewards and motivation for many of the patients.

This was another reminder of what a great job I have, to be able to interact with fans and listen to their stories. In this case with Irv, I was able to find one of the few adults who could adeptly handle their glove.

Irv (Brooks) snagged another one!

One of the more memorable foul balls I have seen occurred during the 2011 season. It was a game between The Rays and the Red Sox that was the ESPN Sunday night telecast. It was a rare game for any number of reasons. The Rays lost 1-0 in 16 innings! The time of the game was almost 6 hours—5 hours and 44 minutes to be precise. (Obviously no pitch clock back then.) Joe Maddon was ejected during the game (we don't see that as much anymore now that we have instant replay, but it still does happen).

During the 8th inning, Sean Rodriguez hit a foul ball that broke a light in the catwalks. Pieces of broken glass showered down onto the field in foul territory near Red Sox third baseman Kevin Youkilis. The game had to be stopped as the grounds crew rushed out to attempt to clean up the broken pieces. As the game proceeded (little did we know that the game was only half over in the bottom of the 8th), the grounds crew returned during the half innings to tend to the field. I am assuming there were no requests from Rays fans for a piece of the glass that Rodriguez hit, but you never know. (*Sometimes fans can be a pane—this one was too easy.*) I do know it was the latest game I had ever left The Trop—I want to say it was around 2 AM!

Stepping out of the box: *If a game goes 14 innings, should we have a second 7th inning stretch?*

2018 Season Poem (excerpt)
90-72 3rd in AL East

We got a hint on Opening Day that this season was going to be fun
When, against Boston we came back in the 8th to score 6 runs!

He pitched his heart out and his stats were the best by far.
We all were relieved when Blake Snell was finally named an All-Star.

90 wins and it was so much fun to watch those victories mount.
But since most of those wins were in Florida, will there be a recount?

From August on the Rays got extremely hot and were certainly cranking
Not bad from a team that early on was criticized for tanking

During those win streaks the Astros/Yankees/Sox and Indians we did drub
Once Tommy came over from the Cardinals he had his own Pham club.

10

Getting My Head
In The Game

A thought struck me during a game in one of my early seasons. At each game, there is a promotion for the fans. There was one in conjunction with Kane's furniture store, to get fans excited about Rays pitchers throwing strikeouts. If during the game the pitchers struck out 10 opposing team batters, fans were rewarded with a coupon redeemable for food. When this promotion started, it was pizza from Papa Johns. After a game with 10 strikeouts fans could take their ticket to one of the Kane's stores in the area and receive a voucher which they could redeem at a local Papa Johns. This was a very popular promotion. How could it not be when you get free food?

The "strike out counter" in the scoreboard area of center field kept track of each strikeout as it was recorded. Even fans who might not have been paying close attention to the game all of a sudden became engrossed when the count reached nine strikeouts. If and when that 10th strikeout was recorded, it became a big deal as the counter flashed out those 10 K's (K is a baseball abbreviation for strikeout, which works great considering Kane's begins with a "K").

In 1859, New York Clipper sportswriter Henry Chadwick introduced the concept of a "box score" to baseball coverage. The English-born Chadwick used the letter "K" to denote a strikeout since he'd already used "S" for sacrifice. (Athlon Sports—10/25/17)

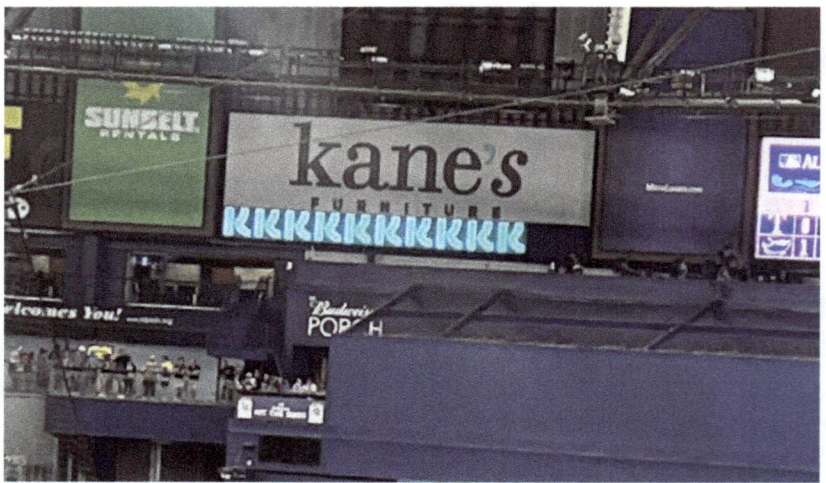

As I observed the fans' reactions and the celebration that took place, it seemed to me there could be even more fun added. Thoughts crossed my mind of what else could be done to enhance their experience at least in the sections where I was working. It had to be attention getting, but also done rather quickly since unless the 10th strikeout was the last out of the inning, the game would still be going on.

Eventually I came up with the idea of holding up a large flag that said PIZZA to further the celebration. I purchased one on eBay. So as soon as that 10th K was accomplished, I would run down the steps to hold up the flag. This idea went over well with the fans, but I was convinced there needed to be more than just a flag.

While traveling with my wife, Jeanette, in Memphis, Tennessee, I came across the perfect accessory to go along with the PIZZA flag. There sitting on a table in a store was a beret type of hat that looked like, yep you guessed it, a pizza! *I tried it on and it fit perfectly, just like Cinderella's slipper... did I just type that!* While wearing it, I found my wife in another part of the store and modeled what would be a much-needed piece to complete the Pizza ensemble. I could not wait for our next game, which hopefully would have those magical 10 Ks to show off my new look.

The Pizza outfit was a big hit with the fans. Once strike three was either swung on and missed, or called, I was off scurrying down those 51 steps in between sections 116-118. Back then I was pretty agile and made it down to the front of the dugout in no time at all (assuming no fan would be *foolish* enough to get up from their seat at that moment of the game). It seemed to me that adding a bit of *ham (uh huh)* on the pizza furthered people's enjoyment of the promotion. People would laugh and even some wanted to take a picture of that goofy Fan Host with the pizza flag and hat on his head. At times, even the crew running the Jumbotron would put the fun pizza celebration up on the big screen.

The Pizza Guy couldn't let the game stop him from celebrating 10K's.

This promotion lasted for a few years, while amazingly gaining a bit of popularity on its own. I was told that back then if you Googled *Rays Pizza guy*, I showed up!

Somehow the MLB Network got a hold of a clip of me going down with the flag and hat. They used it for a piece (not of pizza) they were doing. The segment was asking players throughout the league what their favorite pizza topping was. During the segment, in between players' responses, they included me doing the silly pizza celebration. My nephew was attending a game in Baltimore at Camden Yards when during the half inning, they ran the MLB network pizza bit. He called my wife to say, *"I think I just saw Uncle Bruce running down an aisle on the scoreboard with a pizza hat on his head."*

At the conclusion of the 2013 ALDS playoffs, which The Rays lost to the Red Sox, there appeared an article on ESPN.com. In wrapping up the final game, Gordon Edes was commenting on how many pitchers Joe Maddon had used that game.

To exaggerate his point, he wrote the following: Joe *Maddon summoned everybody to pitch for the Tampa Bay Rays at Tropicana Field Tuesday night. The guy who feeds the stingrays in the Rays' tank. The gyrating grounds crew guy. The security lady who was checking bags before the game found a set of false teeth.*

Any time Maddon touched either arm, even if it was just to scratch his elbow, a new pitcher entered.

Duke Knutson, the press box attendant. Dave Wills, the radio play-by-play man. Don Zimmer.

Maddon used so many pitchers, TBS ran out of commercials.

The guy who waves the pizza flag for free pies for 10 strikeouts.

Dick Vitale, the Rays' No. 1 fan. Ben Zobrist's wife, the anthem singer (bold is my emphasis).
(Gordon Edes, ESPN.com—10/9/13)

Trying to stay current with Longo's theme!

Let the record show that the crazy "Pizza Guy and his flag" stayed current. For those of you that remember, in 2014 The Rays as a team had their own rally cry—*EAT LAST*. This thought came from a book on leadership that Evan Longoria read. The idea being that by winning the last game of the World Series, the Rays would enjoy the ultimate taste of victory by eating last. (It was a great idea and slogan to eat last, but unfortunately for the Rays, that year it became more of a fast.) Once I became aware of this team focus, I had my wife iron EAT LAST in white letters at the bottom of the pizza flag. They are still on the flag to this day. (Of course, I still have the flag...and hat!)

One day I "confessed" to my wife that I had a lingering concern regarding "The Pizza Guy." (The expression on her face conveyed...only 1 concern?) I began to tell Jeanette that I was afraid that one day I was going to run down the steps with the pizza hat on and upon reaching the dugout and holding up the PIZZA flag ,

I would be holding it up backwards and the flag would say AZZIP! I went on to say that I did not want to look foolish. She paused, as only a wife can, then calmly told me that *"I had nothing to worry about, that ship sailed a long time ago."*

The ultimate happened one afternoon when we were going to get pizza. (a fan had given me one of the free promotional cards from the stadium give-away). Here I am in just a t-shirt and shorts, walking across a Papa John's parking lot, when a total stranger yells out, "Hey Pizza Guy!" My wife could not believe it, and all I could do was smile and say hi.

IF pizza was the only thing I wore and waved a flag for, that would be somewhat understandable (at least by some). However, things changed dramatically before the 2015 season. It was during Rays U that I was informed that the pizza promotion was no longer going to take place. Immediately I thought, what, no pizza flag? No pizza hat? You mean when the Rays pitchers now throw 10 strikeouts, I just stand there at the top of my section and do not do anything?

My fears, at least for the moment, were relieved when I found out that the 10-strikeout promotion was still going on. Instead of fans getting a coupon for a pizza, they would now receive a coupon for a mini-sub sandwich (Shortie hoagie) at Wawa's. That is great, I thought. We are still going to celebrate 10 K's. Even though you could not freeze a sub like you could a pizza, to have for a quick meal which many fans told me they did, they would still be able to get a Shortie.

THEN it hit me … where am I going to find a flag that says "SUB?" (I am not even sure I could find one on a naval base.) *Forget the flag for a moment, where have I ever seen a hat that looks like a sub sandwich?* Thoughts were running through my mind at a rapid pace. Not only did I have to change "costumes," but this had to be done rather quickly. It was mid-March and Opening Day was a few weeks away!

I came home from Rays U that evening to tell Jeanette the dilemma I now was facing. The way I was telling her I am sure sounded like The Rays season could not go on because her goofball husband did not have a sub hat and some type of flag to hold up. She patiently listened as the wheels were turning in her creative mind. (Trust me, she is so incredibly creative that she would give Martha Stewart a challenge.)

It was probably the next day or so that she came to me asking me how I would feel if she made a "sub hat"? Of course, I knew not to doubt her creativity, much less her abilities. She went to work on this idea, while still working full time. The finished product was (still is, since of course I kept it) incredible. The detail she put into that hat was unbelievable, but once completed, the challenge was not done. The "bread" was made out of foam, which gave it some significant weight, unlike the flimsy pizza hat. She concluded to hot glue it on one of my Rays baseball hats. The way it was designed and fitted; I had to wear my Rays hat backwards, which provided an even "cooler" element to it. Due to the weight, I had to walk with it much slower since the "sub" overlapped on both sides of my hat. (This shortie was approximately 15 inches long!) I went down the aisles as fast as I could, but felt like I was doing posture training in holding my head so straight and somewhat still. Regardless, it was a masterpiece. This one-of-a-kind homemade sub hat was an even bigger hit than that *store bought* pizza beret.

The incredible homemade "Sub-hat"!

So, the challenge was met, and my wife saved my "bacon" again with her incredible talent. But wait, that was only the hat. What about a flag? *To be honest regardless of the hat, it is the flag that gets people's attention in regards to celebrating the 10 strikeouts.* Without a flag, I am just some "clown" (*I honestly went to "clown college" for a week, with a certificate to prove it. My clown name is Foul Ball!*) with a goofy hat on his head standing by the dugout.

"Foul Ball" driving in style.

First, I needed to have a flag and then I had to decide what to put on it. Again, my superhero wife came to the rescue by making a flag out of blue and white (Rays colors) material. Being the seamstress she is, that did not need as much time as creating a sub. Once the flag was completed, there was still the challenge of what it should read. Jeanette looked at me and said she can make the flag, but I am the "word guy" to figure out what should be on the flag. At best it could only contain 3 words. It needed to be easily read and understood along with having to do with some form Rays baseball and sub sandwiches. I really thought long and hard about this, knowing I had a deadline. Then it hit me, I played it over in my head numerous times before actually verbalizing it out loud. At that moment I foolishly thought it was a "genius idea." (Another one, a pre-*Home Run Derby* inspiration.)

At that time, the Rays were beginning to use a slogan which they still use today, "RAYS UP." It is clever and creative along with being memorable. For it to be still used even today speaks loudly of what a great idea it is. The "RAYS UP" theme was my inspiration for the lettering of the flag. So, I had my wife make and sew on the flag, in bright blue letters, RAYSUB. To this day I am not sure all the fans really got the play on words, but they certainly understood the continued concept of "free food."

For the baseball seasons of 2015 and 2016 upon the 10th strikeout I would "run" carefully with a sub on my head down to the Rays dugout and hold up the flag that said RAYSUB. The fans seemed to take to it once they realized there were no more pizzas coming. Honestly, I believe it was the novelty of seeing a sub hat along with the flag that got their approval. It was still that same goofy Fan Host hoping to bring additional fun and enhance their experience at a Rays game

Balancing the "Sub-hat" wasn't always easy!

At one game, as I was walking back up the steps away from the field just after 10 strikeouts, a young boy, probably an early teenager, came up to me and asked if he could wear the hat for a minute. I had never really thought about that before. In light of all the years I wore the pizza hat, no one had ever made that request. I agreed, as long as he remained right there ... *can't have some "impostor" running around The Trop with a one-of- a-kind sub hat on.* I took a picture or two of him and I believe I posted it on social media as my intern in training.

There was another game that not long after the gates opened,, I saw two young boys, maybe 11 or 12, walking around in banana costumes. The costumes were pulled over their heads, but there was a place for their faces to fit through. I am not actually sure why they were wearing them (like the Pizza/Sub guy should be concerned about what anyone is wearing to the game). They were sitting in their seats by themselves, as they were not part of a "bunch" (sorry I can't help myself). Though they were not sitting in my section, I knew we had to meet: perhaps I could train at least one in being my "protege."

So, I pulled my sub-hat out and went over to say hi. *They looked at me rather skeptically … really kid, you are dressed like a banana at a baseball game.* (Hmm, I think this was in 2016, the same year the Savannah Bananas were founded...is this more than a coincidence?) We talked for a few minutes and I told them that I liked their costumes. Before I left to go back to my sections, I asked them if we could take a picture together. As they remained seated, I stood behind them with the sub-hat on. I still have an oversized copy of that picture hanging on my wall in my study.

During spring training of 2017, it felt like deja-vu all over again. (Thanks Yogi!) The sub-hat and RAYSUB flag were now established, at least in my mind. Then came the news that the sub sandwich promotion had ended. The 10 strikeouts were now being celebrated with a hamburger. One of the national burger chains, Burger King, was now the contributor to the stomachs of Rays fans. 10 strikeouts got you a free Whopper Sandwich Combo Meal coupon upon taking your ticket, still to Kane's.

So, my search began again, for now a burger hat as well as a flag. Honestly, finding a burger hat to add to my hat collection of food items (I also have hot dog and turkey ones too, along with the other hats all inside an official Cracker Jacks vendor bag from Shea Stadium), was really not that difficult. Burger hats are plentiful, unlike a sub hat. So, I quickly secured the needed burger bonnet, but the stickler again became a flag. No matter where I looked there were no burger flags to be found. Shocking huh? By now you know who I went to fix my flag dilemma. Yep, my super seamstress was willing to again come to my rescue. Of course, the challenge was what should this flag say? I came up with a clever saying but nothing "genius" like before. This banner was appropriate to acknowledge Burger King, but did not have a baseball theme. The flag was again in Rays colors of blue and white, along with blue letters that read "KING ME" (get it ... Burger King along with the game of checkers). Jeanette not only made this great flag, but it also included The Rays yellow burst behind the "K." Since this promotion lasted only one season, I do not have many memories of my burger year. Though with a much more manageable hat, I was able to get down the steps faster with my KING ME flag, so there was no *beef* from me (uh huh). Honestly, each year my pace going down is not quite as fast and we will not even talk about the "speed" going back up. (Will the new stadium have escalators ... at least for "senior" Fan Hosts?)

The "Burger Guy" with plenty of ham!

The 2018 season brought a change in menu again. For 10 strikeouts fans would now again go to Kane's to receive a coupon for a free taco, chips and a medium sized drink from Tijuana Flats. From when I started doing my "craziness" in 2012 (though Kane's promotion was already in place at least as far back as 2009), that now meant we had gone from pizza, to subs, to burgers to tacos. Again, this meant another "wardrobe change" along with another flag. If you think about it, obtaining a TACOS flag was not too hard to come by. The flag had (still does) three horizontal-colored stripes (blue, white and red) along with the word TACOS in black lettering. It is easy to spot and certainly gets people's attention upon unfurling it. Now perhaps you are thinking, sure the flag was easy to obtain, but there are not many taco hats floating around. You probably had to go back to your amazing wife again to create a taco hat. That line of thinking certainly makes sense, but you would be wrong. *Believe it or not I already had a taco hat since 2010 (kind of scary huh...)!* I purchased it off of eBay after the All-Star game in Anaheim that year. At that time, I had no idea of what I would ever use it for; it just seemed like a cool hat made out of foam (not nearly as well made as the sub-hat obviously).

The taco hat was a promotional item advertising Taco Bell, which had, and still has, a relationship with MLB. There was one "problem." Taco Bell, was stamped on the front and back of the taco hat. Since it was not Tijuana Flats, I could not go bouncing down the steps promoting the taco giveaway with the wrong logo on the hat. Now this is where Jeanette again came to the rescue. We had a multi sided give away item from The Trop (mini clothes hamper) made out of fabric here in our home that had *Rays* on it. She simply cut the hamper apart and hot glued *Rays* on the front and back of the taco hat. Voila, I now was ready to go. I did find another item that seemed to compliment the taco outfit. They are sunglasses with a jiggling "mustache" that moves with each step I take. Recently, one of the ends of the mustache came unhooked, so I needed to take it home for my wife to repair my "wardrobe malfunction."

"The Taco Guy" became a cartoon character
(artist Elijah D)

I just concluded my 6th season with the Tijuana Flats taco promotion. It seems to me that considering the fan response, this
far and away has been the most popular. Don't get me wrong, all
of the "food groups" that I have worn and flags displayed have
been appreciated by the fans in the stands. Yet for some reason,
there have been more people not only wanting a picture of "The
Taco Guy", but wanting to be in the picture as well. The fans
come out of their seats into the aisle to take a "selfie" or have
someone else take the photo. This includes fans of all ages—

probably the youngest being around 10 up to a woman who was celebrating her 90th birthday. There have been individuals, couples and even a little league team.

Last season on a Friday night, after I had returned up the aisle, a senior female fan approached me. I was beginning to put the taco hat back into the bag (yep, the hat has its own bag, handmade by guess who?) when the fan asked excitedly if she could please have a picture with me and her. One of The Ray Team girls was right behind (*yeah Lauren*) us, so a three-person selfie that included the Taco hat was taken. This was not this woman's first selfie since she knew precisely how to position us, hat and all. The picture came out surprisingly well. After the picture was taken, she told me she needed this for her Instagram.

Before one game, while assisting fans with their tickets a gentleman walked by with a Tijuana Flats polo shirt on. The logo caught my eye and I said to him as he passed, "We love Tijuana Flats here," to which he smiled and said "thanks" as headed to his seat. Lo and behold he was sitting on the far end of the row in one of my sections right at the dugout, but it was not the aisle I normally go down. I then was hoping that the Rays pitchers would come through again with 10 Ks, so I could make my way down to him and his family. When that 10th strikeout was recorded, I made an exception to my usual path. I went down to the dugout and unfurled the TACOS flag right behind him. His wife noticed me first and gestured to him as their family was smiling. At that he got up and asked if we could take a picture together. It came out great, with him helping me hold the flag while still partially being able to see the logo on his shirt. When I asked if they would be so kind as to send me a copy of the picture, his wife agreed. He then gave me his business card, which point I discovered that he was a Vice President at Tijuana Flats.

Also interesting is not only the number of fans who come from other sections (including the club seats directly behind) to meet me at the top of the stairs once I return, but also fans wearing other teams' hats and jerseys who want to take a picture. (I guess tacos break down all team loyalties.) To add to the fun, I ask the fan(s) if in the picture they want to hold the TACO flag with me. This amazingly gets an even bigger response, as if the flag could not somehow be touched by *human hands*.

I get by with a little help from my friends...

Getting my head in the game with these various food promotions has produced some of my favorite memories. It is amazing how a silly costume has produced a lot of fun for not only me, but fans at the game, regardless of the score.

Stepping out of the box: *Can you come to a game dressed as a fan for the opposing team, but then ask a Rays player for an autograph?*

2019 Season Poem (excerpt)
96-66 2nd in AL East
Lost in ALDS 3-2

Stanek/Yarborough were almost perfect against the O's it was a close call
But alas there was no perfect game because there is no Ryne in baseball.

The Trop was packed on the night we played the Angels or often known as the Halos
That seemed appropriate to support Pride night and their rainbows.

Tyler was the dominant pitcher in the AL at the start of the season that was no bull
Once he went on the IL, the Glass-now was no longer full.

The playoff atmosphere here was electric, especially on one memorable play
Altuve was thrown out on the Kiermaier to Adames to d'Arnaud relay.

Cash put Kolarek at 1b during a game with the Giants-no one knew what to say
That series was also strange seeing Longo playing for another team by the Bay.

11

Safe

In my season ending poem for the Fan Hosts in 2014, I wrote the following line:

A grounder to Longo who throws to Zobrist and onto Loney the Rays turn two...

What a great double play, it was a close call, but wait the play is under review.

The introduction of replay and team challenges has certainly added another new element to our game. The umpires who people love to hate, or at least complain about, have been with baseball for as long as we can all remember.

William McClean was the first professional umpire, when he umpired the first game in National League history between Boston and Philadelphia on April 22, 1876. MLB.com

Toward the end of this past season, an older couple came up to talk to me at the top of the aisle. The wife asked if she could go down closer to the field to take a picture of her son who was at first base. At that time there was a pause in the action as the umpires were conferring on a possible play under review. I told her this was a perfect time as the umpires were pausing the game for her to take her son's picture at first base.

She smiled and said, "my son is the first base umpire." Obviously, that was not the answer I was expecting, but I told her to go down since I knew the seat at the bottom of the row closest to the dugout was empty. As she proceeded down, her husband and I began to talk. He was a former little league and high school umpire himself earlier in life. He told me one day his son came home while in high school complaining about umpires, knowing of course that his dad was one. His dad challenged him to see if he could do better, and he accepted. Eventually, after a year of college, he decided to go to umpire school and become a professional umpire. Upon graduation, he worked his way up the ranks of Minor League baseball until he got the call to the Majors about six years ago. He was the only one in his umpire class that has made it to the big leagues! Another one of the perks of this job is meeting great people and often learning their love of the game.

With very few exceptions, and often to our chagrin, the men and women in blue are incredibly accurate. To have to make split decisions with everyone's eyes on you, along with, at times, a game hanging in the balance, must produce a lot of pressure. Though, I would imagine most umpires would say it comes with the job. Have umpires blown a call? Of course, and so have we in life. Despite my frustration at times over a missed call, I still want to see baseball leave the umpiring the way it is. The game (along with life) has become too impersonal, relying on stats, not your gut or individual players at the moment. Regardless of your feelings on umpires, from day one they had to determine if a player was *safe*.

Being a Fan Host, the term *"safe"* has taken on many different meanings throughout the years. It goes way beyond an umpire's call, though I feel I have a pretty good view from where I stand if they would ever need a second opinion.

The first example of *"safe"* comes from the biggest "error" I have ever made at The Trop. It was in 2008, my "rookie" year, but that still is no excuse. In late summer, the Rays were continuing to be the talk of baseball as they kept on winning. That type of success often produces more fans, especially in 2008 when Rays fans had never seen the likes of this type of baseball before. A Saturday afternoon game had a packed Dome cheering on this amazing team. I was stationed down the 1st base line, a few sections further away from where I presently work. It was about the 5th inning when a young man in his late twenties approached me at the top of the section. He was holding a tray full of food and drink. He asked me if I needed to see his ticket. To be honest, I committed more than one error on this play, and it began with my response to him. I told him *yes*; I did need to see his ticket. Now, understand that this is policy for us for reasons I have mentioned previously. Yet, looking back, I should have realized there was no need to check his ticket then.

First, anyone asking you to see their ticket is not sneaking into a seat. Secondly, the game was sold out; there was no room for him to sit but in his seat. Thirdly, by the 5th inning the game was half over. But in my eagerness to do my job, I did ask to see his ticket after already making the errors I just mentioned. He then told me his ticket was in his back left pocket, nodding his head in that direction.

Right there, a few yards past first base though in the stands, I made my biggest error ever. Instead of holding his tray so he could reach for this "unnecessary" ticket, I reached in his back pocket! At the time I never really thought about what I was doing. Immediately I could feel the edge and corner of the ticket as I pulled it out. By now there were several fans waiting behind him to go down, along with fans sitting at the top of the section all watching what was unfolding. So, I pull out in front of all these curious fans, not a ticket, but a *condom*! Yep, even holding it up in the air for everyone to see. I was stunned, embarrassed, and speechless among other things. I quickly put his "ticket" back into his pocket. He asked if he was ok as I quickly waved him down the aisle. Looking back on this incident, when he asked, I should have told him he was "safe."

Some years ago, not long after the gates were open, there was just a sprinkling of fans in my sections. I noticed a man wandering around seats near the dugout, while looking at the lettered rows and seat numbers. He did not seem lost, but as I watched him, I thought there might be some way I could assist him, so I went down. As I approached him, he appeared to be preoccupied with his thoughts and did not seem to notice I was near. Eventually my presence startled him a bit and I asked if he needed any help. He smiled and said no, that he was trying to find a specific section, row and seat, which he had now found. Then he began to tell me his story.

The "found" seats were supposed to be ones he and his son were going to sit in a few months from now. Unfortunately, their plans had changed since his son was being deployed to Afghanistan and would be gone before that game would take place. The dad was looking at the seats while waiting for his son to arrive that night for their replacement game. He was understandably a mixture of emotions, from disappointment to being proud of his son serving to concern over what might happen. We chatted a bit as we moved back to where his seats were for that night's game. When fans enter The Trop, you just never know what their story might be.

A bit later I met his son when he arrived. I thanked him for his service and then excused myself so father and son could have their time together. Their story was a moving one and I found myself thinking about it during pre-game as well after the game started. Through some of that "Fan Host magic," we were able to make the game a bit more memorable for the two of them. Two "camo" Rays hats and a baseball were secured and given to them, which they appreciated. I walked away thinking what a special opportunity The Rays have given me to enhance a fan's experience.

A couple of months later, the smiling face of a fan came my way. I knew he looked a bit familiar, but to be honest, I meet a lot of people on any given game, so it is hard to remember everyone. This fan came right up to me and greeted me like we had met before. Quickly in our conversation, I remembered it was the dad who had the military son who was deployed. He then showed me his phone with his son from Afghanistan was on the screen. I could not believe that I was talking to him, much less he wanted to talk to me at this time when he and his dad should be catching up.

The son was wearing his camo Rays hat and holding up the ball he took with him on his deployment. The dad was back because this was the night of the original game that he and his son were to attend. I spoke briefly with the son who again thanked me for what we did for them at the game they attended a few months ago. I told him he had made my day and thanked him for his service in keeping us back home... *safe*.

One of the best things we do for the fans happens on Sundays. Every Sunday is *Family Fun Day* throughout Tropicana Field. These afternoons are geared toward families making memories together at a baseball game. Depending on where families enter The Trop, there are a number of attractions that immediately get their attention, including face painters, people on stilts and the ever-popular folks who make balloon animals and assorted creations. On many Sunday games there is a special give away exclusively for kids 14 years and under. For about 30 minutes during the pre-game, you can usually find two Rays players signing autographs not too far from their dugout and only for the kids.

I often tell adults looking to get an autograph at any game that if they are unsuccessful, to come back and see me and I will put any name they want on the baseball they are holding.

Once the game concludes, the day is highlighted by kids having the opportunity to run the bases, the same ones they saw the Rays players run on during the game. What a thrill for a child to be able to have that opportunity. Even parents are often in awe just to be able to walk on a major league field. It is a memory making experience that The Rays organization provides for families. Does it take a while? Yes, it does. Probably from the time the game ends to the time the last child dashes to home plate it is about an hour and a half later. Honestly, that makes for a long game for Fan Hosts, especially since most of these Sunday games are at the end of a home stand where we have worked numerous games before. Even simply a weekend series from Friday to Sunday means we work three games in less than 48 hours, including running the bases. Yet, this is one of my favorite things we get to participate in regardless of how tired I am. How do you put a price tag on families making memories together?

In previous seasons, we used to have the kids line up with their families out in hallways on the first base side. (this past season they entered from right field). The line usually starts forming around the 7th inning. Regardless when you get in line, it does take a bit of time to get all the kids through. During many of those seasons, my responsibility was to be on the field by the gate to let people onto the field at section 122. Families would make their way down more than 50 steps in that section to enter the field right across from 1st base. It was there that I would see smiling faces and wide eyes from the kids as they could now see they were close to running. Often parents, once entering the field, would put their hand down to touch the "turf." Knowing that people had been waiting a long time, we tried our best to get everyone through in an orderly and smooth manner. I would thank the fans, especially the children, for waiting as they entered the field.

Positioning myself strategically, I would angle my body at the bottom of those stairs. That way I could see the flow of the kids going toward 1st base while keeping an eye on the fans coming down those steps to prevent them from taking a misstep. There were times that out of the corner of my eye I could see we had a significant gap in the line coming down the steps. As I would turn to look up to see what was the cause of the delay, I purposely would smile broadly. The pause could have been for any number of reasons, from a family struggling with a stroller coming down, or perhaps a grandparent who needed extra time to handle all those steps, to of course a child who was just not paying attention. My intent with my smile was to put anyone who might be causing the backup to be at ease and for them to take their time and be careful.

I will never forget one Sunday when I looked up while smiling to discern the hold up in the line. About halfway up the aisle were parents with their son in front of them who I would say was around 10 years old. As I looked closer, I began to realize what was happening. The son was coming down slowly as he precisely went from one step to another. In his hand was his cane as he was visually impaired. He was making steady progress, but he was slowing the line up as he descended. Obviously, he could not see me, but his parents could as we made eye contact in acknowledging what was transpiring on the steps leading to the field. The parents were there for support, but they were allowing their son to take this challenge on by himself. As he got closer, I was trying to encourage him, but not rush him either.

He finally made it to the bottom step, at which time he then grabbed his cane and extended it to touch the turf. The look on that young boy's face was magical as it lit up knowing he was now on the field. My purposeful smile that I was accustomed to using there was now replaced by one of wonder and joy for this young Rays fan. As he proceeded toward 1st base, his parents went towards home plate to meet their son as all the other parents did. They were letting their son do this all on his own. I, of course immediately stopped the line to allow him all the time he needed. When he reached first base he paused as he placed his cane on top of the bag. Afterward, he was then off toward 2nd base.

As he made his way around the bases, I was mesmerized watching this boy living out his dream that I am sure he had imagined so many times before. By the time he placed his cane on 2nd and headed to 3rd, everyone in the area was aware of what was happening at this special moment. Spontaneously, parents, other kids, the Ray Team and Fan Hosts all began to applaud and cheer. It gave me chills to watch him and still does today as I write these words.

For me, it was as if time stood still as I watched him round third and head for home. That moment was a time I will never forget and I would imagine neither will he. As I teared up, I was so grateful to have been able to experience this special moment as this young boy "energized us all through the magic of Rays baseball." Once he touched home plate with his cane, the roar of everyone was amazing. In so many ways he was *safe* at home.

Stepping out of the box: *Are Dippin' Dots really ice cream?*

2020 Season Poem (excerpt)
40-20 1st in AL East - Lost in World Series 4-2

In the playoffs The Jays were no real challenge, but the Yankees on the other hand
It came down to Brosseau who went deep off Chapman

But we won, we were headed to the Series—all was dandy
A lot of that had to do with a rookie named Randy

Lightning/Rays/Rowdies/Bucs—Champa Bay gave fans a winning itch
I wonder if The Rays will ask Brady to throw out the 1st pitch?

All these champion teams give us fans reason to gloat
Maybe Tom could be in the Rays tank since he knows how to throw from a boat

The media is full of doubts saying the Rays can't compete, not able
Let's not forget there are a lot of 98ers coming out of the stable

The Rays take pride in their defense, seldom a goof
Solid D is a big contributor for home game wins and an orange Trop roof.

12

Alternate Uni's

Growing up as a baseball fan, teams basically had two uniforms (uni's). The home team's uniforms were white and the road team wore gray. Then in the '60s color splashed on the scene with all types of shades and designs. We began to see powder blue or bright green and yellow along with orange among the teams. As the years have progressed, teams have not only added new uniforms, but also unique ones that are worn on special days. *Turn Back the Clock Days* have brought to light vintage uniforms from days gone by. Now, even city or regional styles that reflect the area that the team represents adds another dimension of fun to the game. It is entertaining to see the players in those retro "digs" or now, their City Connect uniforms.

During those *Turn Back the Clock* games, we have seen an assortment of uniforms worn. During those games The Rays have donned uniforms honoring The Tampa Tarpons, The St Petersburg Saints, The University of Tampa and The St Petersburg Pelicans. Lest we forget there were those "faux back" uniforms of The Rays from the 1970's, when, of course the team did not yet exist.

If you trace the uniform evolution of The Devil Rays from the past 25 years, you would find quite a lot of diversity. At their inception there were the purple with rainbow gradient jerseys. Followed by the green and vest style. When The Devil Rays went to become The Rays in 2008, blue and white became the dominant colors, followed by an alternative navy-blue jersey a few years later (2010). Then came the ocean light blue jerseys (2011) that are still worn on Sunday home games.

For the 25th anniversary season of 2023, the organization decided to honor their Devil Rays heritage. They began wearing the vintage uniforms for Friday night home games, and have continued to do so. (Everybody needs to wear some purple now and then.)

In the 2024 season The Rays unveiled their City Connect uniforms that they wear on Saturday home games. The "Grit and Glow" style uniquely reflects the Tampa Bay area and is incredibly popular. The blend of a dark shade of gray, along with the neon colors of purple, lime green and light blue, have caught the attention of fans of all ages.

The style of Fan Host uniforms have changed over the years as well. Before I came on board in 2008, I believe the shirts worn were a Hawaiian style, which certainly fit into the aquatic Rays theme. Then in 2008, as The Devil Rays evolved into The Rays with their new uniforms and The Fan Hosts uniforms changed as well. We wore navy blue jersey style button down shirts with light blue trim. On the front was script writing with white letters trimmed in yellow that said Fan Host. On the back of the jersey, it said RAYS in the logo style with the burst on the "R." Underneath was the phrase *Ready At Your Service* (an acrostic for Rays). This new style was unique, yet still kept us in the baseball theme with the jersey design. Navy blue jerseys were also distinctive in that we were easily visible, which of course is important considering our job.

Then came 2010 when, as I mentioned above, The Rays added

an alternative navy blue jersey as well. It looked great and was a sharp contrast to their home white jerseys. (Obviously they were so good that they are still being worn.) Of course, once those navy blue jerseys were seen, then the fans wanted to wear them, too. That was great from a marketing side, but those jerseys began to impact us as Fan Hosts too. With now more and more fans coming to the games wearing those jerseys, it made us less visible. We now blended in with the crowd and it made it a bit more of a challenge to find us if we were needed, especially in a hurry.

Eventually Fan Host jerseys changed again (2013) to a yellow button-down jersey with navy blue trim. The same script read *Fan Host*; this style was in navy blue and highlighted in light blue and white, with a couple of Rays bursts on them. The back had the same RAYS writing along with the *Ready At Your Service* underneath. These new jersey's certainly helped with our needed visibility. A few years ago, we began wearing a slight "update" where the yellow might be described as The Rays burst color. Now they are pullovers and simply say FAN HOST on the back of the jersey. (see the book cover)

However, during the middle of the season of 2023, we did get an alternate uniform! For those Friday night Devil Rays games, we now have purple jerseys, which reflect the purple from the original uniforms. They are trimmed in a shade of lime green, which again makes us stand out. They are fun to wear on those special nights. (Some of us even found purple tennis shoes to wear with this new uni. Honestly, I bought both a pair of purple and bright yellow shoes to wear on alternate Friday night home games. I even went so far as to switch the laces in the shoes, which gives them an even more fun look.)

Having fun down into my sole.

This 2024 season brought us new Fan Host jerseys with a slight variation. We are still with the yellow jersey look, but we now have a Rays burst outlined in ocean blue on the front. Then on the back of the jersey in the same blue shade are the words FAN HOST.

Technically, some of us Fan Hosts have worn even more in the alternate uni department. As I mentioned in an earlier chapter, The Trop has hosted a variety of concerts, many of which have been in conjunction with a Rays game. Often on those concert games we would have a theme night that correlated with either the music genre or the performer(s). These nights have ranged from featuring a different decade (50-90s), to Country Western Night, Hair Bands etc.

Not wanting to miss an opportunity to have more fun, for me as well as the fans, I have worn an assortment of "uniforms" (costumes) to work a Rays game. I have dressed up like ZZ Top with an inflatable guitar and a long, long white beard; a construction worker (Village People); a Western saloon bartender (Country Western); a Ghostbusters character (80's); a disco dude with a wig, tinted sunglasses and thick mustache; and many more. Coming into the Trop, you do get some interesting looks, but mostly smiles, especially from the fans who laugh and shake their heads.

"...a sharp dressed man."

Then there were those games when *my worlds collided*. On certain theme nights when I had dressed up, we also had gotten 10 strikeouts. That meant the "pizza guy" went down the aisle with his pizza hat on and flag in hand dressed like a Ghostbuster, or a *disco guy*. Those games made for even more interesting looks, much less pictures, that some people have sent me.

I have worn an assortment of wigs, which included, for only a couple of games, a dreadlocks wig for the fact that Manny Ramirez was on the roster (Ramirez only played for The Rays for 5 games in 2011).

As recently as this past season, we had a game on Easter Sunday. I found a pair of glasses with no lenses but had bunny rabbit ears on the top. So, I went around taking selfies with anyone, fan or employee, who was wearing something similar. Just another fun day at The Trop, at least for me and hopefully for them too.

Did someone say Bugs Bunny cartoons?

Certainly, the fans as well, have the opportunity to wear their own "alternate uni's," most of the time with very little effort. On those games when the give-away is clothing, often fans quickly adapt. It is only natural and easy for fans to immediately wear a hat if given one as they enter. Of course, there are those who choose to continue to wear the hat they came with and hold on to their new lid. Others will wear the new hat on top of their old one, but all in all, hats are very easy to accessorize.

There are other clothing giveaways that make it a bit more challenging. If it is a t-shirt, jersey or hoodie, you will find a significant number of people simply putting it on over what they were wearing. Then there are the ones who want to look just "right," so they go to the restroom and change.

Even adults got into wearing the Flappy Boi Hoodie this past season.

Putting something on your head took on a new look in 2018 when The Rays gave away DJ Kitty heads. (Yep, a full size mascot head. You can still purchase one on eBay. I just saw one for $33- with free shipping!) Then the question for fans was, do I wear this head now during the game? I was not at the gates where they were given out, but I am pretty sure most people probably immediately tried it on and then took it off. However, there were kids who decided to wear it the entire game. Periodically they appear at a game a few times each season.

The ultimate challenge for wearing alternate uni's came in 2017, when at the gate, fans were given a DJ Kitty onesie! This one size fits all "uniform" caused even more decision making to be made. Yes, there were fans, again, mostly younger, that made the ultimate commitment. They went into the restroom as themselves but exited outfitted in full DJ Kitty garb. Personal confession, after briefly trying both head and onesie on, they are both extremely warm. As *cool* as they are, they became one of the very few items I probably will not wear at The Trop.

Speaking of giveaways (from the classic fedoras to the eyebrow raising Wil Myers bike horn), for a number of games my first couple of seasons, I gave them out at the gates. Please know from my personal experience, and I can only imagine all the years since, that "we" have seen and heard it all. It is amazing the tales people will tell to get their hands on a giveaway that is only for kids 14 and younger. They range from, "I left my sick child at home to I have a friend who teaches 12 students in an out of state school." Then there are the older adults who bend down to appear to be smaller, but they do smile as they cringe to get back up. Or the older kids who still claim to be "14," however, they have significant facial hair and just put their car keys in their pocket.

I have heard of some serious negotiating going on once a child receives a kid only giveaway that some adults covet. The astute adult will see certain kids who just aren't interested in the giveaway, but took it since it was handed to them. They politely go over to the child and show them a $5 bill in exchange for the desired souvenir.

Matt Garza was a pitcher for The Rays for the 2008-2010 seasons. He played a significant role in the World Series run as he was the ALCS MVP. On July 26, 2010 he became, and still is the only pitcher in Rays history to pitch a no-hitter in a nine-inning game. What a fun game to watch. He walked one batter, who was erased on a double play. In his no-hitter, Garza only faced the minimum of 27 batters.

Garza had a goatee, which gave him a distinctive look. One evening, before the game in which he was to pitch, a season ticket holder came up to me. He had glued a small goatee on his chin in honor of Garza. It was kind of funny. He told me that he had this idea of wearing it every time Garza would pitch. As a matter of fact, he thought it was such a great idea that he wanted his girlfriend to wear one as well when they came to the game. Guess what? She did not think it was as great of an idea as he did. She refused, but told him to give the extra goatee to Bruce—he'll wear anything (ahh nice to have a reputation among fans at The Trop).

Lest you think otherwise, of course I wore it! Really, it was a blast to put it on every game Garza pitched, whether that season ticket holder was there or not. (I had some extra adhesive for my clown nose—remember my clown "college" experience as *Foulball*—so a simple dab was all it took.)

Garza Goatees

Finally, since I was known for wearing costumes in the theme of the concert, a friend of mine at church asked me in front of everyone what I was going to wear for the next concert where the group was ...

"Barenaked Ladies"!

Stepping Out of the Box: In a Father's Day promotion back in 2014 dads were given a James Loney BBQ grill set. Thoughtful, but shouldn't the player associated with the promo have been a pitcher, so to grill *sliders?*

2021 Season Poem (excerpt)
100-62 1st in AL East
Lost in ALDS 3-1

731 consecutive times the result was the same
Until last season when Yarborough threw a complete game

222 homers, dazzling defense and strong bullpen the strength of
the team really shows
In all of those stats from last year don't forget 106 RBI's from
Austin Meadows

At the beginning even fans had to wear masks unless for drinks
or eats
Along with sitting socially distanced by zip tied seats

Randy was the Rookie of the Year that we enjoyed here in the
Dome
The highlight of his season was in the playoffs when he stole
home

We said goodbye to Ozzie/Brosseau/Wendle and others through
dealings and trades
But let's trust the front office so we can have our own boat pa-
rades.

A big off-season acquisition was Corey Kluber
Let's hope he picks us up and delivers just like Uber

13

Closer

As I mentioned in the beginning of the book (*Opener*), both my wife and I started working as Fan Hosts at the opening of the 2008 season. I never dreamed it would last so long, much less be so much fun. My mind was blown immediately that first season. As the Rays continued to win, so many people were shocked. I vividly remember after another victory during the season looking up numerous times to read the AL East standings posted on the Jumbotron. I would just stare in disbelief. This was not some win streak or even getting "hot." This carried on as the season progressed. The Rays were the talk of baseball, going from worst to first in a shocking way.

Before the season had even started, my wife and I had planned a vacation in October. We were taking a cruise down the west coast of the US and Canada. We would leave out of Vancouver and eventually end up in San Diego, with various stops along the way. I remember Jeanette, at more than one time during the season, asking me what would we do IF the Rays made the playoffs? *Playoffs? Are you kidding me? Playoffs?* (Channeling my Jim Mora voice for you who are old enough to remember that NFL classic quote.)

Honestly, they were not the exact words I used with her, but I reminded her that the Rays had never finished 500, much less gone to the playoffs. As the season progressed and the team kept winning, that vacation question was becoming more and more relevant.

The unthinkable became a reality on Saturday, September 20 in a victory over the Twins. For that game I was up in the Party Deck in left field. I would walk around those packed stands reminding the fans how many outs were left in the game. The excitement was building and culminated when Longoria went down in foul territory and caught a pop up. The Trop exploded, and I was fortunate enough to be there to witness that amazing event. THE RAYS WERE GOING TO THE PLAYOFFS!

The ALDS had the Rays playing the Chicago White Sox. They won that series 3-1. The Rays were swimming in uncharted waters. Not only had they never been to the playoffs before, but they also had never won a playoff game, much less a series. I was super pumped that the Rays were now headed to the ALCS, but we had a flight to catch the day after game 1 of the series. I could not believe this was happening, in so many ways.

So, after working the game 1 loss to the Red Sox, we headed to Canada the next day. I vividly remember working that first game out in left field. As the game ended, and as the Rays fans were walking out, there was an obnoxious Red Sox fan waving good-bye as the fans exited. I was honestly surprised nothing happened between the fans. (I did think of him and wondered what he was doing after the Rays won game 7!)

We flew to Vancouver and arrived in time to see The Rays win game 2 on that famous slide by Fernando Perez in the bottom of the 11th inning. Since we had never been to Vancouver before, we had scheduled to fly out early before our cruise actually left. Thanks to a gracious concierge in our hotel, they let us watch games 3 and 4 in a private lounge which no one was using. Obviously, we saw less of Vancouver than we had originally thought, but watching those two games was priceless.

Game 5 brought the first of many interesting twists for us for the remainder of the series. Our youngest daughter, Kelly, was living in NYC at the time. Through her friend's father, they were able to get seats for game 5 in Fenway. So, off they went on the train to watch the Rays potentially clinch a spot in the World Series. If you remember, the Rays blew a big lead and the Red Sox came back to win, forcing at least game 6 back at The Trop. My daughter told me even though the Rays lost, it was one of the most exciting sports events she had ever been to.

There was a travel day between games 4 and 5 and we had made our way down the west coast. One of our ports of call was Seattle. We went over to the Seattle stadium to take a tour. When we were on the field, a coach walked by doing some training, and he kicked a ball over to my wife. (Hmmm *what happened to that ball? I know we used it for some pictures we had taken back on board the ship in our Rays gear, two of which still hang on my office wall today*.) As we went through the team store, they were selling off items from an old scoreboard. There was probably an 8-foot sign that said *Tampa Bay*, that I thought about buying (key word was *thought*). Since I never asked my wife, and I was pretty sure it would not fit in the overhead compartment of the plane, as well as not knowing where I would put it once we arrived home. I did not purchase that sign. But I still thought about it.

...but will it fit in the overhead compartment?

The day we docked in San Francisco was also the same day that game 6 was to be played in St. Petersburg. I received another call from our NYC daughter saying she was going to fly home to watch the game at Ferg's with her friends. She obviously knew we were not home, but she also knew where the spare key was. It was later that day when I received a second call from her that I realized her plans had changed *slightly*. Upon arriving home, she was able to not only secure a ticket to the game, but through a friend, the ticket was in what was called back then The Whitney Bank Club (you know, the one with food and drink included).

As we talked, I was feeling good about her fortune getting tickets for game 5 at Fenway as well as game 6 at The Trop. She told me she hoped that The Rays would win that night. I thought duh ... of course you do, until she told me that she also had a ticket to the Bucs game the next day. It was then that, at least for about 24 hours or so, I secretly wanted her life!

Our itinerary for the cruise called for us to have an overnight stay in San Francisco. So, instead of eating on board the ship, or even at one of the nicer restaurants in town, we found ourselves looking for a sports bar to watch game 6. It was late afternoon on the west coast for the evening game at The Trop. We found a good sports bar not too far from the ship. Obviously, there was s not that much interest in a game between the Rays and the Red Sox in San Francisco, much less late afternoon on a Saturday. So, we went in with our Rays gear on and our cowbell, I (Yeah we packed one), I was hoping to be able to see the Rays clinch, and maybe see our daughter on TV. Well as you probably know, we did not see the Rays win (they lost 4-2) nor did we see our daughter. However, as we were watching the game, one of our friends who lived in St. Pete walked in. He was working for NBC as a cameraman for the upcoming Presidential election and was covering one of the candidates. He had the night off and came to watch the Rays, too. Even that good fortune did not bring the Rays any luck either.

I left that sports bar discouraged. Not only had the Rays lost forcing a game 7, but our ship was pulling out of port right about the time the game would be starting tomorrow night. The next morning, while still in San Francisco, we headed to the new Giants stadium where we had signed up for a tour of the ballpark as well. (Can you believe what a trooper Jeanette was to be putting up with all of this baseball?) After the tour, while still out front, my phone rings. Guess who? Yep, our Kelly, who was still headed to the Bucs game that afternoon, but had also, believe it or not, had a ticket to game 7, again, in the Whitney Bank Club. So, besides being even more envious of my daughter, I still had to face the reality that as we would be pulling out of the port of San Francisco at the same time game 7 would be starting. Not only was I not there, I could not even watch it.

Remember this was 2008, so internet and phone service were not what they are today. As the game began, we were sitting down in the main dining room for dinner. I had my phone nearby, hoping to hear any updates from Kelly. The longer the game went on, the more anxious I got. Finally, I had to excuse myself from dinner with a table full of people. I could not take the tension anymore and I certainly was not hungry.

Every once in a while, I would get a score from Kelly, but that was limited, at best. Back then, the ship for a while was still able to access ESPN. Even though the game was not being carried, there were scrolling scores at the bottom of the screen from all games which had or were taking place on Sunday, including the NFL. I paced those decks over and over again, like an expectant father. From what little I knew, the Rays were winning, but any details, including the inning, I was unaware of. I am not sure of the time lapse between when Aoki stepped on second base and put that ball in his pocket and when I finally got the news. Honestly, now all these years later, I do not even remember if I found out the final score on the TV screen or from Kelly on my phone. Regardless, I am pretty sure I let out some type of scream or yelled in one of those hallways of the ship. To think in my first year as a Fan Host the Rays were going to the World Series and I missed seeing it by only about 3,000 miles!

We did celebrate that night, along with putting a sign on our cabin door saying "World Series Bound." Then the wheels in my head started to spin. The next day our cruise we headed to Monterey. On our excursion, we stopped at Pebble Beach Golf Links, where

I had my picture taken with a doorman while switching hats so that he was wearing my Rays hat.

From St. Pete Beach
to Pebble Beach

After Monterey, we had a day at sea before finally docking in San Diego, which was the day of game 1 of the World Series. So, *I thought* that we could get off the ship early in Monterey. Then we could catch a *red eye* flight home which would be tough, but we would be back in time to work the first game of the World Series.

I thought this was a pretty ingenious plan. Jeanette, who was also a Fan Host, had gotten caught up with the Rays this season, as well as ALCS while on the ship. So, I now had to share this genius strategy with her. Once I laid out my master plan of leaving the ship early and flying home, she calmly stated, "*I don't know about you, but I am staying onboard until the end of the cruise.*"

It just didn't seem the same. I missed Jeanette not flying home with me. I really did!

YEA right, I might be foolish, but I am not as dumb as I look, even with a taco hat on!

WE both flew home out of San Diego on game 1 of the series. When we boarded our flights, I asked the flight attendants if they could talk to the pilot about relaying the score of the game over the intercom. They were nice enough to do that, but alas it was disappointing news with that game 1 loss.

Game 2 found us both working. It was very exciting to be in a World Series atmosphere. (My only other World Series experience was when I went to game 2 of the 1969 series between "my" Orioles and the Mets. If you are a baseball fan, you know I do not need to say anything more.) The Trop that night was electric with excitement, and as you probably know, The Rays won. Unfortunately, that was their only victory in the '08 series. However, I humbly take full credit for that victory!

Examine the facts. My first season as a Fan Host, the Rays not only finished the season over 500, but they made the playoffs. Not only did they make the playoffs, but they went all the way to the World Series. Then they only win one game, which is precisely the only Series game I worked as a Fan Host. It just seems undeniable, right?

Wow, 16 seasons later, I would have never imagined I would still be a Fan Host (or more accurately that The Rays would still put up with my goofiness.) These years have been some of the most fun I have had in my life, along with meeting some of my favorite people of all time. Hopefully this book has touched your heart in some way, or brought a smile or two to your face. The next time you come to The Trop, stop by and say hi. Or better yet, come and sit with me in either section 116 or 118. Who knows, you might end up holding up the TACOS flag or wearing the Homerun Derby! Regardless I think you will agree with me that *There Is No Place Like Dome.*

Stepping Out of the Box: Should you come to a baseball game wearing the jersey from another sport?

2022 Season Poem (excerpt)
86-76 3rd in AL East
Lost WC 2-0

A combined no-hitter lost in the 10th was a complete turn off
Who would have guessed we would come back and win on a KK
walk off

The lockout caused the season to be delayed, definitely not nice
Because of it the Rays played the Blue Jays 5 games in 4 days,
twice

Remember that time in The Trop, the tension was insane
When Rasmussen in the 9th lost his perfect game?

Isaac Paredes added pop to the lineup which we gave thanks
Who could forget his three-homer night here against the Yanks?

With Phillips gone, through the roster The Rays had to sort
Until a new position player was found to pitch, which was Bethan-
court

Extra Innings

Stories submitted by fellow Fan Hosts
from around The Trop

"David, a now 20 year old man came looking for me. His tickets were in section 108, and he asked about the "guy that gives out baseball cards." He was told I was on the 200 level. He asked Dennis the 200 even side lead if he knew of the 'guy', Dennis directed him to where I was 208-210. He approached me and asked if I gave out baseball cards, when I replied in the affirmative he said "I gave him a card when he was much younger and that he remembers looking up the player. (I always have cards on me and it goes like this "hey kid, want to make a deal? If I give you a baseball card of an old time baseball player do you promise to look him up and read about him? 999 out of 1000 say yes I then add "the other part of the deal is if you come to another game you look me up and tell me what you have learned about him, deal?) He is now playing at a D2 school in South Carolina and is having fun. He asked if I had another one to give him and I obliged by giving him a Roberto Clemente card (we were playing the Pirates). This is one of many that have come back to tell me about the player, albeit they usually come back the same year, sometimes the same day."

Eddie Madden

"In the first three years I worked at gates a lot. One year I was at Gate 1 on a regular basis and often handled the door down towards the end where season ticket holders would come in. I had an older couple come through my line with their tickets on their phone, but their screen was cracked and had black spots through it and it was difficult to scan the barcode. After working with it with no success they mentioned that others had tried but had never gotten it to scan. I kept working with it and eventually got it scanned. I suggested to them that they needed to get a new phone. Over the course of the year on several occasions they sought me out at the gate and had me scan their phone since they decided that I was the only one that could get it scanned. I was always able to scan it after getting the hang of it but would each time suggest a new phone. Finally near the end of the year they came through my line at the gate and made a point of showing me that they had in fact gotten a new phone and it was now easy to scan their tickets. I congratulated them on their upgrade."
Dennis Slattery

"Typically, I work Section 203-205 during games. We do not have a Fan Host in all the voms on the suite level so we focus on the sections that have the most fans in them. And, because I am often needed elsewhere, Section 203-205 can more easily be monitored by a Fan Host in 205-207 while I'm away tending to other matters.

From time to time, I get young parents and their children in the front rows. Over the years I've noticed that the kids and their parents are ill prepared for some of the things that can happen when sitting in the front row - especially when it relates to foul balls coming into the area. Hence, I typically give these fans what I refer to as a pre-emptive warning. Basically, I let them know they are sitting in Foul-Ball-Territory and that the lefties are the ones we have to be most watchful for (as they are more likely to hit a foul ball over the netting and into our Section). Depending on the situation I sometimes talk directly to the child - making sure their parents are listening, too.

One game, not too long ago, I was observing a mother who had brought her young son to the game. They were sitting in the front row and the little boy had his baseball glove on - and the game had begun. My guess as to his age? He was 4, maybe 5 years old. So, I went down and gave them one of my pre-emptive warnings. I spoke directly to the little boy and his mother was listening intently. After telling him to be most diligent about the lefties, I turned to his mother and asked if he understood what I meant when I referred to the left-handed batters.

Without hesitation, the mother looked at me, shook her head yes and announced, "Yes, my son understands, he's a switch-hitter!"

I found this very funny because knowing what I know, most kids at that age don't know their right hand from their left hand much less know if they are better hitting from the left side or the right side!!!!"

Steve Yost

"I was standing at my vom when a little boy, 5 years old approached me with a cell phone in hand and said "excuse me sir".

I asked how I could help him and his reply was "could you please turn the noise down in here because I can't hear my cartoons".

I apologized and asked where he was sitting. He pointed towards the top row where his parents were chuckling.

I walked him back to his parents and his dad immediately asked if his son had asked me to turn down the noise. I told him that was exactly what he asked.

Both parents laughed and his mother proceeded to tell me they had him at the movies the previous week. In the middle of the movie the little boy stood up and promptly asked aloud if they could "please pause the movie because I have to go to the bathroom". His mother said he received a lot of laughs from the other patrons.

Kudos to the parents. It appears they have raised a very polite little boy with a tremendous sense of humor."
    John Bailey

"In September 2019, I was working as a Fan Host Lead over the third base line for a Tuesday evening game between the New York Yankees and Tampa Bay Rays, when I was approached by a young couple who were attending the game. They were asking questions about the stadium as they had recently moved to the Tampa area. They also mentioned that the wife was pregnant with their first child. As we continued to talk, prior to the start of the game, I found out that like myself, the husband was a huge Cal Ripken Jr. fan. They had agreed to naming the child, which they had just found out was a boy, after the great Orioles shortstop.

I found out where they were seated and after the game started, I picked up a couple of souvenirs for their yet to be born son. I gave them a "First Game" certificate for them to remember the game, as it was technically, the first MLB game that their son attended. I also gave them a navy blue, child's size Tampa Bay Rays cap and a used MLB baseball. During the time that I was gone, they had decided that they wanted to announce the gender of the baby to their friends and family over Facebook. I suggested they allow me to take their photograph from behind home plate, during the game and that they write the name of the baby on the "First Game" certificate. This way they could post the picture, along with any other information they planned to share. They loved the idea and really appreciated me helping them with their name and gender reveal. They plan to call him, "Rip".

 Helping folks have memorable experiences is what makes this job even more special. Although young Rip did not get to see any of that exciting game on that Tuesday evening (won by the Rays on a Ji-Man Choi walk-off home run in the 12th inning), I am sure he has been told about his night at the Trop!"

Frank Krebs

"Having been a Fan Host for many years, there are quite a few memories that come to mind. Since there doesn't need to be an appendage to Bruce's book, I will share one that resonates with me and drives me to elevate fans' experience in the area I work.

One average baseball night, a family of 12 from 3 generations-were coming into my section. They were so excited to be at a Rays game, experiencing it for the very first time all together. After chatting with them for a bit, some sat down, while some went to explore the stadium. I said to them, 'When you're all together, please pull me aside so we can get a great family picture!'

The game and the night went on. As they were leaving, I reminded them about the pictures and they exclaimed, 'We totally forgot!' With that, I took a bunch of group shots on one of their phones.

That baseball season ended, and the next season began. One night, a woman approached me during the game and asked, 'Nancy, do you remember our family from last year? You took our family's picture-the one we almost forgot to get.'

I responded that I absolutely remembered them. The woman continued, tearing up, 'Well…my Dad, Grandpa, suddenly passed a short time after the game. It's been so hard losing him. But we wanted to thank you. That was the very last picture we had taken together. It was such a happy day for all of us. Now, that picture is a precious memory to us, Nancy, thank you.' Tears filled my eyes, and we hugged for a bit.

I am so grateful for the opportunities I get to make a cherished, baseball memory for those who come my way…You never know who that might be."
   Nancy Nickel

"I don't remember the year but, in the beginning of the tenth inning of an extra inning game I jokingly went down a few rows and said to the fans "ok. I'm here to collect the extra inning fee you only paid for 9 innings" a fan said that's ridiculous I'll go home. I had to tell him I was joking even as the fans all around were laughing. (they got the humor)"
   Eddie Madden

"At Tropicana Field, I witnessed a random act of kindness tonight. A young man with special needs in my section would stand up with his hand in the air while each team was pitching throughout the night. A gentleman with his family in the section next to me further down purchased an autographed baseball from the fan store and handed it to this young man. Brought a tear to my eye as well as others around me!! The young man was so excited 8/24/2018 "
   Patricia O'Neil

The Allure of the Orb

It was a busy night in Left Field, with my fair share of little gloved boys eager to get an Arozarena practice ball "tossed up" in-between innings. There were a pair of brothers, probably 6 and 8 years old, that I paid a bit more attention to. After every 3rd out, even if Randy wasn't headed towards left field, these two kids hustled back-and-forth, trying to predict where that magical ball might be headed. At one point late in the game, the older boy made a great grab to acquire his gift. The 6-year-old was dejected, head lowered, as he slowly made his way up the stairs and back to his seat. "Now, now's the time!", I thought to myself, remembering the batting practice ball I grabbed before the gates opened. It was secure in my back pocket, anticipating when it would meet its new owner. With only an inning left, I walked over to the seats where the boys and their father were sitting, bent down and asked the younger boy, "Did you ever get a ball tonight?" "No, and my brother won't even let me hold the ball he caught", he said sadly. I reached into my pocket and replied, "We'll, here you go", as I handed him the ball. He briefly gazed at it, looked up and said, "thank you". His father also thanked me and I told them they were welcome as I headed back to my section. A few minutes later, the father walked up to me and said, "He might not have seemed excited about getting that ball, but he's really happy you gave it to him. Thank you." After the game, the father thanked me again as they were leaving. It's amazing that the gift of a cowhide covered ball can provide so much joy for young fans ... and Fan Hosts too. It's just the allure of the orb."
  Kip Kedersha

"We were assigned a new supervisor in the 300 section. He was brand new to the Rays and I saw an opportunity to haze him. He was talking to another lead getting instruction when I walked up to him and said "Boss I have an issue you need to write up. The fans are complaining that the hydraulics of the cat walk in CF is not working; they can't see the lineups on the scoreboard." He proceeded to the desk and wrote it up on his supervisor sheet he turns in after every game. Funny is funny."

Eddie Madden

"Hi Mr *Dan Walsh,*

Good evening
I'm T. M.
Do you remember me?

Thank you for Last week. I was very happy I could meet you this time. Your kindness made me a wonderful memory. That will be in my memories forever.

But I'm so sorry I can't speak English. I wanted to talk to you about Rays more. Since the 2019 season, I am waiting I can go to Tropicana field again. This time I was very exciting. And I appreciate you introduced me your friends. I am so happy I could meet you and your friends.

Jack and Mary are very kindness too.

I appreciate your kindness and support for three games. Monday I returned to Tokyo Japan. Mr Dan Thank you again It's the memory of a lifetime. Everyday I watch Rays game on MLB com TV. Go Rays May I meet you again?

I am looking forward to going to Tropicana Field next season too. About My iPhone.I appreciate you help me Thank you again."

Sincerely T. M.
Tokyo Japan

"On June 24 Friday night it was raining Nina and Diane were at gate 1. I (Nina) was putting the fans wet umbrellas in the bags. Diane was handing out towels to the fans that got wet from the rain. The fans were so surprised that we would do that for them. The fans were saying you guys are so nice for doing this.

So we decided to have a little fun with the fans. as we were handing out towels and umbrella bags we said, "Hors d'oeuvres will be served shortly. Coffee and cake will be served at 9:00." The fans had a good laugh."

Nina and Diane

"After a game, a group of fans came down to the top of the black seats of Home Plate Club. They asked, "Can we take a small sample of dirt from the warning track right behind home plate?" I chuckled and informed them that it was artificial turf ... .and "No, you can't take a piece home." I then invited them down to check it out for themselves. We all had a good laugh."

Gregory Graham

The Astro Abduction
"It was a normal gameday at the Trop. David Price was pitching for the Rays. At that time, he had a French Bulldog named Astro. Astro was very well known to Rays fans, as Price brought him several times to spring training, to the field during the regular season, and to Fanfest. He even made appearances in the dugout. So popular was this dog, that the Rays made him into a giveaway which was a Price figurine holding Astro. David began a tradition, or superstition of sorts, of putting the Mini Astro figurine on top of the dugout every time he pitched. He even made a shelter out of a red solo cup and cut a little door in the side to keep plastic Astro from the elements.
On this particular day, all was well until a fan sitting near the

dugout decided he was going to dive on top of the dugout, swipe Mini Astro and put him in his pocket. I immediately went to him and asked him to give it back. He looked at me as if I was crazy and said, "Give WHAT back?" I told him I saw him take plastic Astro. He denied it once again. The fans around us were all telling me they saw him put it in his pocket as well. I explained to him that it was Price's "good luck charm" and that he put it on the dugout every time he pitched, and when he noticed it was gone, he would be upset. Well, he denied that he had it once more. Just then, the inning ended and David was coming off of the mound. As he approached the dugout, his face dropped and he was motioning to the red solo cup where Astro had been but was no more. I pointed to the man with the dog in his pocket and said, "It's in this man's pocket". Price gave him a stern look and that's all it took. Astro was saved. I was a hero."

Jean Brennan

"It was late in the game one week night and we had just gotten 10 strikeouts so that the Kane's promo was triggered. I went down my aisle between innings and on the way back up a fan stopped me and asked me how she could get her free sofa. Being confused by the question, I asked her what free sofa? She said that they had said that if the team gets 10 strikeouts every-one in the stadium wins a free sofa. I explained to her that in fact you win a free taco combo. Her response condescending to me was "Kanes doesn't sell tacos." I explained that she would go to Kanes with her ticket and she would get a coupon for a free taco combo at Tijuana Flats, but she was certain that she had won a free sofa and was not accepting any other explanation. I suggested that she check with guest services at gate 3."

Dennis Slattery

(Author's note: *As a follow up to this encounter we now joke and say if 10 strikeouts provides a sofa, then say 7 strikeouts will simply be a night table, where 15 will be an entire bedroom suite!*)

"I always enjoyed my hosting shift at the Trop when I was stationed at the main gate rotunda. The excitement of fans arriving was energizing and the anticipation of a good game to fill their day, brought me joy. The hustling crowd at times, however, seemed somewhat overwhelming, but, a smile and warm welcome from the fan hosts seemed like inviting home family to a reunion if only for a few hours.

Such was my assignment, one busy Saturday afternoon, when I noticed a well-seasoned fan, long in years, shuffling slowly straight towards me with a confused look on his face. I must admit my heart strings were plucked abruptly for his countenance reminded me of the look of aging family members who couldn't quite clearly put thoughts together any longer. He looked me straight in the eye and declared…" I can't find my phone number". My thoughts turned to concern, as my eyes scanned the crowd looking for a missing companion for this dear man. "I can't find my phone number," he repeated. 'Would you like me to call someone for you, 'was my panicked response. Again, the same declaration…" I can't find my phone number". Now I was scanning the crowd for some help, where was my lead, or should I perhaps call security.

As he drew closer and closer to me, his statement got more intense. Stopping directly in front of my face, he said "I can't find my phone number, can I have yours?" A sly smile emerged from his weathered face as his partner of many years came scurrying up to our conversation. "Leave that young lady alone" was her message, "We've got a game to get to." He left with a smile, her arm linked in his and my mind stamped with a sweet Fan Host memory."
Jeanette Reynolds

2023 Season Poem (Excerpt)
99-63 (2nd in AL East)
Lost Wild Card 2-0

The season began with more records than DJ Kitty.
The way the season ended truly was a pity.

A weak schedule to start the season the media complained
99 wins later no one uttered again that refrain

In honor of Harold Ramirez, autism received its due
We supported the effort wearing on our heads wigs of blue

Arozarena further made a name for himself that every fan knows
From RandyLand, HR Derby Final to of course his famous pose!

The 25th anniversary made us think of seasons and players of the past
Those statues of Aki and Longo will make sure those memories last

To make the playoffs teams have to play great
The Rays have made it 5 years in a row and 9 times since '08

15

Call To The Bullpen

One of the unique aspects of our beloved game is that it is the only sport where the bench players reside in two different areas. Think about it, in football or basketball or hockey, those not playing are either sitting or standing on the sidelines together. But in baseball, we have a dugout for some of the reserve players, and we also have a bullpen. This is where most of the relief pitchers are positioned, along with a few other players and coaches who sit while watching the game.

Along with this unique feature and environment, equally unique is its origin and name. There isn't one! There are a number of theories regarding the term *bullpen,* but no one can seem to agree on just one. The theory that intrigues me is that the relief pitchers used to warm up in an area with Bull Durham tobacco ads, hence the name bullpen. For the sake of this book, since we are focused on The Rays, their AAA team plays in Durham and is called the Bulls. I am going with that one.

In baseball, a call to the bullpen means the team needs help and assistance for any number of reasons.

My personal bullpen for this book contains a number of people. However, the leader, the number 1 *reliever* who has recorded more saves than all the others combined is my wife, Jeanette. As you have read throughout this book, she has *saved* me even from myself. As I stated earlier, this adventure started with us together becoming Fan Hosts in 2008. She worked a number of years while still holding down a full-time job. Finally, she did not feel she could continue to do both jobs well. Jeanette wisely decided to keep her full-time employment. There are, of course, a lot of obvious reasons she made that correct decision, but to boil it down to one, she chose *cash over Cash* (well really Maddon was still manager when she stopped).

Yet, she continues to encourage me as I keep going to The Trop. (Let's be honest, from what you know of me after reading this book, wouldn't you also want to "send me off" for a couple of hours to get me out of the house?) As you have read, her seamstress abilities furthered my "career" in the 10 strikeout promotions. She has listened supportively as I come home after games—whether pumped over a victory or down trodden when I had a bad game in some form or another. Foolishly, I worked the night of our 43rd wedding anniversary. That "error" did not stop Jeanette from surprising me and coming to the game, along with cupcakes that we shared with the fans.

I love her deeply for loving me for who I am, craziness and all! She has always been my number 1 fan in all of our married years together. Plus without her constant encouragement, this book would have never become a reality.

My bullpen required a specialist, to which my daughter Kelly (yes, the same one who's 2008 postseason experiences I envied from afar) responded immediately, as well as enthusiastically. She got me out of jams with my document confusion, along with designing the front and back covers, among other things. Kelly is a marketing guru. Her expertise in how to promote the book was invaluable in getting this book into your hands, literally from cover to cover!

The two All-Star relievers Kelly and Jeanette.

I made another call to my bullpen for help from my friend, Kathy Saunders. Kathy is the editor of *The Bay Magazine* for the Tampa Bay Times. During Covid, Kathy wrote an article about Rays baseball being missed, that included me.

Scan the QR code with your phone to read the article

I *pitched* (yep again) her my idea for this book during a Rays game. She and her husband, Joe, were sitting in their seats by the dugout in 118. Through the years I have watched their family, specifically their children, Joe (now a scout for The Seattle

Mariners) and Julia, grow up on Rays baseball at The Trop. I asked Kathy if she would be willing to assist me with my book, and without hesitation, said yes. I knew her "veteran experience" would be invaluable for a "rookie" like me.

Julia and I "grew up" together at The Trop...well Julia did, many still question when I will grow up...

Also sitting in my bullpen, who I constantly have *warming up*, are the Fan Hosts who, for most of my career worked on either side of me. These patient people not only have done their Fan Host responsibilities extremely well, but had to put up with my shenanigans right next to them. This includes going above and beyond their duties at times during the games, when I am up to my craziness. My deepest thanks to Patty Mulligan, Cynthia Bordas, Nancy Nickel and Dennis Slattery for their friendship and their ability to *hold* it together.

Everyone "nose" to be a Fan Host you must be well "red."
Sidekicks Nancy and Patty.

Seated in the bullpen are the following Fan Hosts who con-
tributed their stories found in The *Extra Innings* chapter. Their
reflections provided additional *relief,* as well as adding another
dimension by hearing what they have experienced. Therefore, my
sincere appreciation goes to Eddie Madden, Jean Brennan, Gregory Graham, Nina Lutz (and Diane), Dan Walsh, Kip Kedersha,
Steve Yost, Frank Krebs, Patti O'Neil, John Bailey, Dennis Slattery,
Nancy Nickel and Jeanette Reynolds for *answering my call to the
bullpen* for enhancing this book.

My bullpen is getting crowded, but there are four other "relievers" who I need to thank too. For the most part, these people
have served as my Leads throughout my tenure at first base. Jen
Funk, Bill Shane, Bruce Poli and Ken Jones have been more than
supportive of me during my antics. They have given me flexibility
in doing my job, as well even adjusting the break schedule so I
could be around when potentially the 10th strikeout was recorded. Thanks, to all of you for letting me be me!

The bullpen would not even have existed if it were not for The
Tampa Bay Rays Organization. By hiring me as a Fan Host I have
learned about baseball, people, life, and certainly myself. Specifically, thanks goes out to Eric Weisberg (VP Fan Experiences)
who joined the organization and headed up the Fan Hosts the

same year I was hired in 2008. Eric is responsible for developing the culture of Fan Hosts that has made us one of the best, if not the best group in MLB. He and his staff have allowed me to not only *Get My Head In The Game,* but to *energize our fans through the magic of Rays baseball,* at a special place called The Trop.

16

Off-Season

Photo by Charlie Bergh

"We are safe. The roof blew off the part of the Trop."

I woke up on October 10 at around 3:45 AM to the above text. Most of my family and I had evacuated to North Carolina to avoid hurricane Milton. Upon reading that text, I tried to go back to sleep, but could not. So around 4 AM, I turned on the TV to see what had and was still transpiring at home. By then, Milton had blown through Tampa Bay and was on his way to Orlando. I scanned numerous channels trying to find an update on how people and property were doing. After about 45 minutes, I saw my first video footage of The Trop. Immediately I was stunned, as I tried to grasp what I was seeing. Tears formed in my eyes as the drone footage played over and over. My "friend" of over 25 years had been severely wounded.

The loss of lives or the destruction to people's homes and businesses are much more significant than the damage to a stadium. Upon eventually hearing that family and friends were safe, I found my grief increasing for that Dome that I had grown to love.

None of us, especially me, would have guessed that something happening once the baseball season was over would have such an impact on our lives, our homes, our community and even this book. At this time, no one knows the ultimate fate of our beloved Trop. Regardless, I hope, even more this book has brought back memories, perhaps a smile, and if you are like me, even a tear or two. I am convinced now even more "There Is No Place Like Dome."

Meet Bruce

Bruce Reynolds finished his 16th season working as a Fan Host at Tropicana Field. He is married to his high school sweetheart, Jeanette. They have two amazing daughters, along with four fabulous grandchildren. Bruce is a graduate of High Point College (University), Gordon-Conwell Theological Seminary and The Mooseburger Clown Arts Camp.

Bruce has been a public speaker for over 50 years. His career has included arena announcing, radio broadcasting and along with speaking to groups ranging from 10-1000+. This has included teams in MLB, NFL and the NBA, as well as church and civic groups. Feel free to contact him if you are interested in an interview or having him come to speak about his book.

fanhosts@gmail.com

www.ingramcontent.com/pod-product-compliance
Lightning Source LLC
Chambersburg PA
CBHW051201120626
46547CB00012B/1151